PARTICIPANT'S GUIDE

AUTHENTIC SECURE TRUSTED REAL INFLUENTIAL

FREED TO LEAD

EFFECTIVE IDENTITY-BASED LEADERSHIP

Rod Woods and Steve Goss

Published by
Freedom In Christ Ministries International
4 Beacontree Plaza, Gillette Way,
Reading, RG2 0BS, England
Email: office@freedominchrist.org
www.freedominchrist.org

ISBN: 978 1 913082 26 0

First edition 2023

Acknowledgments

Contents

Enjoying the course?
You'll love the *Freed To Lead* book!

Freed To Lead by Rod Woods is the accompanying book for the course. It goes into the topics covered on the course in more depth and covers a host of related topics too.

Order from your local Freedom In Christ office (see page 8), the shop at www.ficm.org.uk or www.ficm.org or your usual supplier of Christian books.

Why Take Part In *Freed To Lead*?

A company of great Christian leaders could change the world for Jesus as they extend God's loving rulership into every area of society. Our deep desire is for *Freed To Lead* to help raise up that company of great Christian leaders, one of whom might just be *you*.

We have faith that you can become a great leader. You might be a great leader already. You might just be starting on your leadership journey. Or you might not yet be certain that God is calling you to leadership at all. But we have confidence that you can become better and better as a leader. We may not know you personally, but we know our God who lives in you.

Although many people may not consider themselves as "leaders", everyone will have to lead at some point in their lives. Whether it's in the workplace or the home, the church or the community, everyone will have to lead. For some people this thought is exciting. For others it is terrifying! What many Christians don't realize is that God has already given us all we need to become the leaders we need to be. *Freed To Lead* will help you discover what God has already given you as a Christian and how to apply it in any leadership context you find yourself in.

Many give up leading because it gets tough and painful. They have not been prepared for the challenges of leadership. Many leaders – great leaders – think they are failures when they are actually making a massive difference in the lives of people around them. We have developed *Freed To Lead* to help you understand the challenges of leadership and then overcome them.

If you are a leader already then you will know that all leaders want to be the best they can be. But the truth is that you can read as many "how-to" books as you like and still not be a truly effective leader. People don't follow leaders who simply use the right techniques. They tend to follow leaders who are authentic and real. *Freed To Lead* will help you discover how to lead as the person God has made *you* to be.

Christian leaders have a huge advantage over others because they have become new creations in Christ. As Christians, we not only have a new identity in Christ, but through Christ we have received significance, security, and acceptance from our heavenly Father. You probably know these things already as a Christian. This course will help you to take the truths of this new identity much deeper so that you can learn to lead as the new person in Christ that you are.

We call this approach to understanding leadership "identity-based leadership". Identity-based leadership involves leading as the person God has made you to be rather than trying to lead based on someone else's model or someone else's book. Identity-based leadership frees us from drivenness and burnout. It enables us to survive personal attacks and use conflict positively. It also enables us to overcome other barriers to effective leadership.

In short, *Freed To Lead* will help you understand the person you already are in Christ so that you can become the leader God created you to be.

A Note On Language And Spelling

As *Freed To Lead* is on sale internationally, we have consciously tried to avoid language that will not work in all English-speaking contexts. Rather than picking either American or British spellings, however, we have chosen to vary it. In this Participant's Guide we have used British spelling. In the accompanying *Freed To Lead* book we have used American spelling.

How To Get The Most Out Of *Freed To Lead*

Engaging in all the various components of *Freed To Lead* will enhance your learning experience and ensure that you receive the maximum benefit.

- Do your best to attend each session. Be sure to catch up with any you have to miss (perhaps by borrowing the DVDs if available).
- Each session contains a Bible study (in the "Word" section of your notes). If this is not covered in your group session, do take the time to work through it each week on your own or with a friend, ideally before the corresponding session.
- Participate fully in all the discussions. Take the risk to be open and vulnerable with others on the course. Much of your learning will come from the other people on the course with you as together you digest the course content.
- Record any faulty beliefs you become aware of on pages 188–189. You will be taught how to renew your mind (Romans 12:2) to resolve them.
- Actively seek to apply what you learn from each session. We would encourage you to find one or two things that you can use practically in the next week. But be wary of trying to do too much all at once.
- Ensure you take the opportunity to go through *The Steps To Freedom For Leaders*, a kind and gentle process that will help you "do business" with God on leadership issues. It starts on page 133 and is designed to be used once you have gone through the ten course sessions. One of the best ways to go through the Steps is with one other leader. An equally good way is on a day away with your fellow course participants.
- Read the book *Freed To Lead*, by Rod Woods. It contains much more detail than we could provide in the course. It also covers many more topics not included in the course (see page 4).
- Join the "Freed To Lead" group on LinkedIn (see page 8): connect with other leaders; ask questions of the authors; discuss the teaching.

We pray that God will multiply the effectiveness of your leadership and make you confident to lead as a new creation in Christ Jesus!

Connect With Us!

Join Rod Woods and Steve Goss on the Freed To Lead interest group on LinkedIn.

- Ask questions
- Join in discussions
- Connect with Christians in leadership

From LinkedIn, search for "Freed To Lead".

Get the Freedom In Christ Ministries app

- Daily devotional direct to your smartphone or tablet
- News and prayer requests from around the world

Search for "FICM News" at your app store.

Join the Freedom In Christ Facebook group

- Instant updates on what's happening in the world of FICM
- Share your Freedom In Christ stories

From Facebook, search for "Freedom In Christ Ministries", select the "closed group" and ask to join.

Find your local Freedom In Christ website

We operate in around 40 countries. Find your nearest office or representative at www.ficminternational.org.

- Our US site is at www.ficm.org
- Our UK site is at: www.ficm.org.uk

Register on our UK site to receive our daily devotional by email.

SESSION 1:

The Adventure Of Leadership

WELCOME

- What is the greatest personal challenge you've faced?
- What was the outcome?

Read Psalm 37 out loud in your group, without comment.

Pause for a quiet moment of reflection on the content of the psalm.

Read

- Read 2 Timothy 1:1–14
- Read the passage again and make a list of the five most important words from the passage. Why do you think they are important?

Understand

- Who wrote this passage?
- To whom is this passage written?
- Why was this passage/letter written?

Discern

- What do you think is the gift of God that is in Timothy? (verse 6)
- What do you think it means to "fan into flame" this gift of God?
- What has God not given us? What has God given us? Why has God given us this? (verses 7–8)

Apply

- As a leader, what is the gift of God that is in you?
- What do you think you might do to "fan into flame" this gift of God?
- Why do you think Paul emphasized that God has not given us a spirit of cowardice?
- How would you describe "the spirit of cowardice"? What does it look like in leadership?
- How do power, love, and self-control counteract cowardice?
- Why are power, love, and self-control important for leaders?
- In light of this passage, what might you expect as a leader – both positively and negatively?

Commit

- In your leadership, when have you experienced "the spirit of cowardice"? Why? What did you do when you were faced with this cowardice?
- In light of this passage, what might you do as a leader when faced with cowardice?

Purpose Of *Freed To Lead*

To enable Christians to lead confidently from a vision of Christian leadership based on our identity in Christ.

> Pause For Thought
>
> **Throughout this course, we will give you many opportunities to discuss your own thoughts and ideas about leadership. When we use the word "leadership", we all assume that we know what we're talking about. So let's consider the following questions:**
>
> **What is "leadership"?**
>
> **What makes a good leader?**
>
> **Which of the two questions was more difficult to answer? Why?**

The Bible And Leadership

The Bible is our foundation for understanding leadership.

In *Freed To Lead* we will **not** reduce Jesus or the Bible to

- a set of principles
- a private morality
- a surface covering of worldly styles of leadership.

Christian leadership is <u>the</u> leadership the world really needs today – not just the Church.

Leadership Is Tough

For this reason I remind you to fan into flame the gift of God, which is in you through the laying on of my hands, for God has not given us a spirit of cowardice (that comes from anxiety) but of power and of love and of self-control.

(2 Timothy 1:6–7, our own translation)

Why Is It So Difficult To Lead – Especially For Christians?

Leaders feel like failures

No adventure is easy – adventures test our stamina and courage

Struggles in leadership do not indicate that something is wrong with you

But understand this, that in the last days there will come times of difficulty.

2 Timothy 3:1

Why Leadership Is Tough

People are **overwhelmed by**

- Change
- Challenges
- Choices

People are **overloaded**

- Information overload
- Choice overload

People are **unfocused**

- Without a coherent worldview
- Without a strong set of values
- Without a focus

People are **undisciplined**

- Lawlessness
- Changing morality

People are **anxious**

- Broken society
- Unstable
- Hopeless, expecting loss

Leaders feel **disempowered** and **demoralized.**

The Leadership Dilemma

In each session we will consider a "Leadership Dilemma".
A dilemma is a challenge with no straightforward solution.

Our society needs real, effective leadership. Such leadership is the only way we can resolve the great issues of our times, whether they are personal, social, economic, or global. Yet the very people who need true leadership are the ones who consciously or unconsciously undermine, attack, sabotage, and destroy leadership.

Pause For Thought

Take a moment to review your own perspectives about the times in which we live as leaders. Discuss the following questions:

Do you agree that it is difficult to be a leader today? Why or why not?

Have you experienced resistance to your leadership? What effect has this had on you?

As a leader, do you generally feel encouraged or discouraged? Why?

The Message Of Freedom In Christ

Know the **truth** of who you are in Christ:

A saint – a holy one

Significant

Accepted

Secure.

Be aware of the reality of the spiritual world and resolve spiritual issues with **truth.**

Be transformed through the renewing of your mind with **truth.**

As Christians, we have a great leadership advantage. Jesus Christ, the greatest leader who ever lived, lives in us by the power of the Holy Spirit. Jesus has destroyed the power of sin, death, and hell in the cross and the empty tomb.

WALK IT OUT

What action(s) will you take in the coming week to apply what you have learned?

Pray for those who are feeling discouraged as leaders.

Pray for one another's leadership challenges.

For further information on the topics covered in this session, see the accompanying book, *Freed To Lead*, by Rod Woods, chapters 1 and 2.

Your Leadership Journey

Throughout *Freed To Lead* you are encouraged to create a timeline of your leadership experiences. The purpose is to help you reflect on your leadership experiences – both positive and negative – so that the concepts presented in the course can be applied to your leadership context.

You can complete your timeline on the next page. If you need more space to write, simply copy it out onto a separate sheet of paper.

At this point, record your first experiences of leadership – at school, at church, in sports, in family life.

Progress to your first "professional" or "official" position of leadership – first job, position at church, leading a club or team.

Who were influential leaders you followed as you were developing as a leader?

You will come back to do more work on the timeline in future sessions of *Freed To Lead*.

First experiences of leadership

First "official" position of leadership

Subsequent positions of leadership

Current position of leadership

Who do you lead?

What do you do?

Who are you as a leader?

Potential future position?

Influential leaders

Memorable successes

Times of conflict or disappointment

Hopes and dreams for this position

Signs of the health of your system

Periods of personal anxiety

Periods of systemic anxiety

Potential pitfalls

Goals to transform your leadership

SESSION 2:

Real Christian Leadership

WELCOME

- Who would you consider to be the greatest leader in all of history?
- Why?

Read Psalm 37:1–4.

Express your trust in the Lord. Praise God by expressing His goodness and delightfulness.

Read

Read Luke 22:24–27, John 20:19–23, Luke 12:42–48, John 10:10–15, Galatians 4:1–7.

Understand

Create a one or two word title for each passage. Write it under the reference in the chart below.

Discern

For each passage make a comparison – what does the passage say about Jesus? What does the passage say about the disciples/us?

	What does it say about **Jesus**?	What does it say about **us**?
Luke 22:24–27		
John 20:19–23		
Luke 12:42–48		
John 10:10–15		
Galatians 4:1–7		

Apply

- What do all five passages have in common?
- Based on these passages, in what ways are we like Jesus? In what ways are we different?

Commit

- Which metaphor best describes your current style of leadership?
- Which metaphor might reveal a weakness or lack in your leadership?

In light of these passages write a list of statements about who you are because of who Jesus is, for example, "Because Jesus was with us as one who serves, I am like the least, as one who serves."

WATCH

Every single one of us can be a real Christ-centred leader. In this session we will consider the nature of true Christian leadership and what makes it distinctively different from other forms of leadership.

Pause For Thought

We will start by considering a key question when it comes to leadership.

"Leaders are born, not made." What do you think about this statement? What does the Bible have to say about it?

Our response to the statement will say a lot about how we understand leadership in general and Christian leadership in particular.

The Nature Of Real Christian Leadership

Servant: *A dispute also arose among them, as to which of them was to be regarded as the greatest. And he said to them, "The kings of the Gentiles exercise lordship over them, and those in authority over them are called benefactors. But not so with you. Rather, let the greatest among you become as the youngest, and the leader as one who serves. For who is the greater, one who reclines at table or one who serves? Is it not the one who reclines at table? But I am among you as one who serves."*

Luke 22:24–27

Sent One: *Jesus said to them again, "Peace be with you. As the Father has sent me, even so I am sending you."*

John 20:21

Steward: *And the Lord said, "Who then is the faithful and wise manager, whom his master will set over his household, to give them their portion of food at the proper time?"*

Luke 12:42

Shepherd: *He who is a hired hand and not a shepherd, who does not own the sheep, sees the wolf coming and leaves the sheep and flees, and the wolf snatches them and scatters them.*

John 10:12

Son: *So you are no longer a slave, but a son, and if a son, then an heir through God.*

Galatians 4:7

Real Christian Leaders:

- Are followers
  "Follow me, and I will make you fishers of men." Matthew 4:19

- Believe that the Bible is the Word of God and live accordingly

- Have a genuine relationship with God

- Are grounded in the reality of who they now are in Christ

- Are being led by the Spirit of God and growing in the fruit of the Spirit

- Are becoming more and more like Jesus in character.

Christian leadership is an issue of discipleship. If we are not following Jesus well, we won't lead others well.

Christian Leadership Is:

the interactive relational process

of influencing people and people-systems

towards beneficial outcomes

through

your identity,

character, and

calling in Christ,

using

your God-given strengths

and spiritual gifts

as well as

your talents,

skills, and knowledge.

The Definition "Unpacked"

Process – ongoing, never fully complete

Relational – people-centred, not task-oriented

Interactive – expect to be changed, not just to change others

Influencing both people and people-systems – individuals as well as groups and organizations

Outcomes – the "fruit"

- Economic
- Social
- Environmental
- Personal
- Spiritual

Identity – who you are in Christ

People will follow who you are and how you are before they will follow what you do or say.

Strengths and spiritual gifts – God has called you and supernaturally, uniquely gifted you.

Are leaders born or made? The answer is both!

Talents, skills, knowledge – leadership is not only **who you are** but also **what you do**.

Excellence in leadership demands focus on your strengths and delegation in your "weaknesses."

Definition Of Christian Leadership

Christian leadership is the interactive relational process of influencing people and people-systems towards beneficial outcomes through your identity, character, and calling in Christ, using your God-given strengths and spiritual gifts as well as your talents, skills, and knowledge.

Pause For Thought

So we are called to lead, whether or not we are a "natural" leader! Discuss the following questions:

How has this session challenged or changed your perception of leadership?

What has been the most important concept for you in this session and why?

How does "Christian" leadership differ from the world's understanding of leadership?

The Leadership Dilemma

We tend to think that becoming a better leader is all about improving our leadership style or trying to look like what we think a "natural" leader looks like. However, those are not the things that will make us great leaders.

Real Christian leadership can transform society. It is the type of leadership that every organization everywhere needs.

Our vision is to see genuinely Christian leadership not just in homes and churches but all over the place, to see Christians being so obviously great leaders that they are in demand everywhere.

WALK IT OUT

What was the outcome of your action item(s) from the last session?

How will you apply what you have learned during the coming week?

Pray for one another to become the leaders God desires.

Reflect on your own leadership experiences using the leadership timeline on page 18:

- What memorable experiences and successes do you recall from your past leadership?
- What conflicts and/or disappointments arose in those past experiences of leadership?

You will be encouraged to work through *The Steps to Freedom For Leaders* at the end of this course. But if something in this session has prompted you to want to examine your identity as a leader more closely, you might like to look at Steps 1 and 2 now (pages 138–150).

For further information on the topics covered in this session, see the accompanying book, *Freed To Lead*, by Rod Woods, chapter 3.

How To Connect With Freedom In Christ's Discipleship Teaching

You don't have to have gone through Freedom In Christ's core teaching to do *Freed To Lead* but it helps. Here are some ways you can get to grips with it:

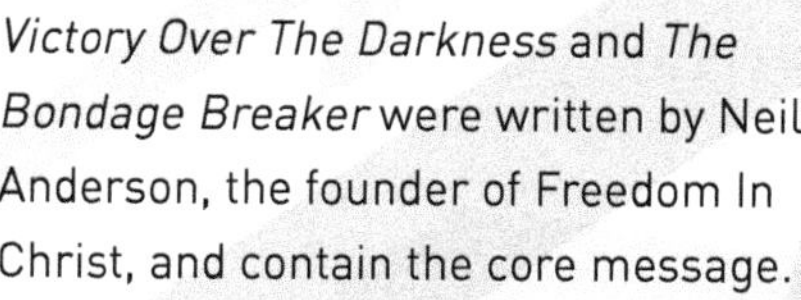

Victory Over The Darkness and *The Bondage Breaker* were written by Neil Anderson, the founder of Freedom In Christ, and contain the core message.

The Freedom In Christ Course by Neil Anderson and Steve Goss has been used by over 250,000 people around the world.

Steve Goss wrote *The Discipleship Series*, four concise, straightforward books that contain the message of *The Freedom In Christ Course*. Their titles are: *Free To Be Yourself*; *Win The Daily Battle*; *Break Free, Stay Free*; and *The You God Planned.*

The Grace Course by Steve Goss, Rich Miller, and Jude Graham contains the core message of Freedom In Christ with an emphasis on understanding the grace of God in our hearts not just our heads.

The Steps To Freedom In Christ by Neil Anderson is the ministry component of our core teaching. A kind and gentle way to get rid of "rubbish" from the past, it has been used by millions around the world.

Get further information at www.ficm.org.uk or from your local Freedom In Christ office or representative (see page 8).

SESSION 3:

Being And Doing

WELCOME

- If you had a chance for a "makeover" in life, what would you do differently?

WORSHIP

Read Psalm 37:5–8.

Wait silently before the Lord for several minutes.

Thank God that He will act on your behalf and that he will make your righteousness and justice shine.

WORD

Read

Read Galatians 5:13–26, Luke 6:43–45.

Understand

- Who wrote the passage from Galatians? To whom was it written?
- Why was this passage/letter written?
- Who is speaking in the Luke passage?

Discern

- What is the opposite of "the Spirit?"

Make a comparison chart on the following page by listing the fruit of the Spirit and the work of its opposite.

The Spirit	The ________________________

- According to Galatians 5, what is your calling?

Apply

Compare and contrast the theme of the passage in Luke with the passage in Galatians:

- How are the themes of the passages different? How are they the same?
- Why are the "works of the flesh" like "devouring" one another?
- How do you "walk by the Spirit?" Why is it important to "walk by the Spirit?"
- Where does "good fruit" come from? How do you cultivate "good fruit"?

Commit

- Do you think leaders are more or less likely to give in to the flesh?
- When have you given in to the works of the flesh? What keeps you from walking in the Spirit? Ask God for forgiveness and commit to a pattern of walking in the Spirit.
- What are the treasures of your heart? How have they produced good fruit in your leadership?

We are wired to "do" and we naturally assume that our behaviour is the primary issue. Yet the primary issue in both discipleship and leadership is not doing: it's being.

Pause For Thought

We tend to learn a lot from other leaders, especially those we have followed ourselves. They can make an indelible mark on our lives.

What is the best experience you've had with a leader?

Why was it so good?

The Pharisees' Leadership – A Focus On "Doing"

"Do you not see that whatever goes into the mouth passes into the stomach and is expelled? But what comes out of the mouth proceeds from the heart, and this defiles a person. For out of the heart come evil thoughts, murder, adultery, sexual immorality, theft, false witness, slander. These are what defile a person. But to eat with unwashed hands does not defile anyone."

Matthew 15:17–20

"They are blind guides. And if the blind lead the blind, both will fall into a pit."

Matthew 15:14

Your doing will always flow from your being.

BEING

Identity, Character, Calling

A unique person

- Mind
- Will
- Emotions

A unique temperament

- Introvert or Extrovert
- Thinker or Feeler

A unique background

- Culture
- Gender
- Upbringing
- Experiences

A unique make-up

- Natural abilities
- Strengths
- Weaknesses

DOING

Actions, Choices

Making choices

Taking action

Building relationships

All leadership involves both who you are and what you do. If your being is not right, your doing will not lead in a healthy way.

The Advantage Of Being A Christian Leader

If your being is right, your doing will lead in a healthy way.

Enemies Of Real Christian Leadership

The World Can Hold Us Back

The world encourages us to look to our status or position to get our sense of worth.

To the degree that we base our identity in our leadership position, our leadership will be distorted, dysfunctional, or less effective.

People will follow **who you are** and **how you are** before they will follow what you do or what you say.

God is not measuring you by your job level, the size of the team you lead, the outward trappings of success, or any other external factor. He has just one concern: your character – whether or not you are becoming more and more like Jesus.

The Devil Can Hold Us Back

"In your anger do not sin": do not let the sun go down while you are still angry, and do not give the devil a foothold.

Ephesians 4:26

I gave you milk, not solid food, for you were not yet ready for it [literally: able to receive it]... since there is jealousy and quarrelling among you.

1 Corinthians 3:2

The Bible is clear that when we sin we give the enemy a **foothold** in our lives, a place from which to operate.

The battleground is our mind, our thinking.

Submit yourselves, then, to God. Resist the devil, and he will flee from you.

James 4:7

The Steps To Freedom In Christ (see page 30) is a process to help you remove the footholds of the enemy and ensure that your being is healthy.

The Flesh Can Hold Us Back

We can try to lead in our own strength – thinking the outcome depends on us. We'll become angry and frustrated as we fail and blame ourselves or other people.

The key issue is knowing what is really true and making a choice, moment by moment.

> *Live by the Spirit and you will not gratify the desires of the flesh.*
>
> *Galatians 5:16*

> *Do not be conformed to this world, but be transformed by the renewal of your mind.*
>
> *Romans 12:2a*

We must make a habit of renewing our mind, uncovering the lies we are prone to believe and replacing them with truth.

Stronghold-Busting

Determine the lie you have come to believe

What effect has believing it had in your life?

Find as many Bible verses as you can that state the truth and write them down.

Write a prayer/declaration

- I renounce the lie that...
- I announce the truth that...

Read the Bible verses and say the prayer/declaration daily for 40 days.

Character Is The Key

Leadership is essentially a discipleship process.

A disciple is "someone who is learning to become more and more like Jesus in character."

The evidence of growing in character is an increase in the fruit of the Spirit in your life that will show in your actions.

> *But the fruit of the Spirit is*
>
> *love,*
>
> *joy,*
>
> *peace,*
>
> *patience,*
>
> *kindness,*
>
> *goodness,*
>
> *faithfulness,*
>
> *gentleness,*
>
> *self-control;*
>
> *against such things there is no law.*
>
> *Galatians 5:22–23*

Maturity is:

- an increase in willingness to take responsibility for your own mind, will, and emotions (soul) and make good choices
- an increase of love for others and a want to serve them in humility
- an increase in consistency between the internal and external – "what you see is what you get" – that others will experience as integrity.

Brokenness And Fruitfulness

> *So to keep me [Paul] from becoming conceited because of the surpassing greatness of the revelations, a thorn was given me in the flesh, a messenger of Satan to harass me, to keep me from becoming conceited. Three times I pleaded with the Lord about this, that it should leave me. But he said to me,* ***"My grace is sufficient for you, for my power is made perfect in weakness."*** *Therefore I will boast all the more gladly of my weaknesses, so that the power of Christ may rest upon me. For the sake of Christ, then, I am content with weaknesses, insults, hardships, persecutions, and calamities. For when I am weak, then I am strong.*
>
> *2 Corinthians 12:7–10*

Part of God's preparation for real Christian leaders is brokenness.

We never experience the power of God in our lives unless we are brought to "an end of ourselves."

God might use:

- Loss of reputation
- Personal conflict
- Injustice
- Health issues
- Financial difficulties.

His purposes are:

- To get to the issues needing to be resolved
- To move us to the place of knowing that we are dependent on Him
- To strip away those things which we have made to be substitutes for God
- To restore the intimacy of our relationship with Him.

Leadership Also Involves Doing

All leadership involves both who you are and what you do. Your doing flows from your being – ALWAYS!

Deciding

- Acting in faith
- Making the choice.

Discerning

- Recognizing God's best for people and people-systems.

Directing

- Giving vision and mission
- Keeping an eye on the big picture.

Developing

- Promoting health in people and systems.

Delegating

- Sharing authority with responsibility.

Disciplining

- Creating shape and form
- Training with focus and correcting behaviour if necessary.

Criteria When Considering A Leadership Style Or Theory:

- Is it consistent with the Bible?
- Does it flow from the leader's being?
- Is it appropriate and beneficial for the context and situation?
- Is it wise?

The Leadership Dilemma

Jesus said: *"I can do nothing on my own."* John 5:30	Paul said: *"I can do all things through him who strengthens me."* Philippians 4:13

We can have a tendency either to forge ahead and do things in our strength, or to hang back too much and not do what we should. The biblical principle is: I can do "all things" but only "through him who strengthens me".

Pause For Thought

In this session, we have introduced a concept that may be new to you: how our being as leaders shapes our leadership.

How do you understand the difference between being and doing in leadership?

How important do you think your "style" of leadership is? Why?

How has the world, the flesh, or the devil held you back in leadership? How will you overcome this?

WALK IT OUT

What was the outcome of your action item(s) from the last session?

How will you apply what you have learned this week?

Pray for one another in your leadership responsibilities.

Reflect on your own leadership experiences using the leadership timeline on page 18:

- Describe your current leadership position. Who are you as a leader? What do you do? Who do you lead?
- What are your hopes and dreams? What are signs of health in your context?

For further information on the topics covered in this session, see the accompanying book, *Freed To Lead*, by Rod Woods, chapters 4 and 5.

SESSION 4:

Leading In Your Context

Which Old Testament person do you most identify with? Why?

Read Psalm 37:9–13.

Thank God that wickedness and wrongdoing shall not prevail.

Thank God that His people will inherit the land – that is, become people of influence throughout your city, region, or nation.

Read

Read 1 Corinthians 12:12–31.

As you read, make note of the words "one" and "many" or "all".

Understand

- Who wrote this passage?
- To whom is this passage written?
- Why was this passage/letter written?

Discern

- Metaphorically, in this passage what does "the body" represent?
- What do the "parts of the body" represent?
- Which parts of the body are given greater honour?
- Why do you think God has made the body in this way?
- How does the suffering of one member of the body affect the whole body?
- How does the honouring of one member affect the whole body?

Apply

- How would you describe the corporate culture of the Corinthian church?
- What things tend to affect "the body" both positively and negatively?
- Describe what it feels like to have a blister on your foot. How does it affect the way you walk? What do you think might be the spiritual equivalent of having a "blister" on your "walk"?
- What is the spiritual equivalent of having a "blister" on the body of Christ?
- Describe a time when someone under your leadership was suffering. How did the group suffer? How did you suffer?
- What do you think would be the effect of "a member" being separated from "the body"? How would this affect the individual member? How would this affect the body?

Commit

- Describe a way that you could honour another part of the body to which you belong. How do you think this might affect the whole body?
- When have you felt separated from "the body"? What were the circumstances surrounding this? How did it affect the group you lead?
- How can you reconnect to the body?

WATCH

A leader who has been successful in one place can fail in another leadership context – and vice versa.

> **Pause For Thought**
>
> **Sometimes it seems that leadership is a mystery. We simply don't know why we might seem to succeed one time and then seem to fail another time.**
>
> **When do you find it easiest to lead?**
> **When do you find it difficult to lead?**
> **What makes the most difference between the two?**

People-Systems

System: a set of things working together as parts of a complex whole.

- A computer system
- A digestive system

People-system: a set (group) of people with a connectedness from which its own identity and form emerge. It develops a common sense of identity and way of doing things.

- The human family
- The biblical term "household"

Why People-Systems

People-systems always influence the behaviours of the people within them. They govern :

- Organization, identity, and ways of relating
- Personal satisfaction and meaning
- Conforming behaviour

People-systems will influence us even more than we influence them.

Leaders In People-Systems

The biblical word for leaders of people-systems is "**steward**".

All people-systems have leaders. Some form of leadership will always emerge.

- If we behave like a leader and people follow, we are leading, regardless of our title.
- If people do **not** see us as leader or do **not** follow, we are **not** leading, regardless of our title.

People-Systems As "Persons"

Brain

The leader is like **the brain.**

- Through our *being* we regulate healthy functioning of the people-system.
- Through our *doing* we help the people-system make good choices and take wise actions.

Our *being* as leaders influences our people-systems more deeply and profoundly than we realize. It is our primary leadership influence in our people-system.

Spirit

The **spirit** of a people-system: an invisible reality which influences and affects people within its range socially and spiritually.

The spirit of a people-system operates in accordance with spiritual principles:

- Sin and legalism bring death to the spirit of the people-system.
- Repentance and forgiveness bring life to the spirit of the people-system.
- If we sow to the flesh in a people-system, we will reap corruption.
- If we sow to the spirit in a people-system, we reap life in the people-system.

The past influences the present in the people-system.

Soul

The **soul** of a people-system: the emotions, the mind, and the will.

- Emotions or "emotional processes" of a people-system are:

  The complex interplay of

  - Impressions
  - Feelings – especially liking and disliking

  All of which influence

  - Thoughts
  - Emotions
  - Choices.

- The mind of a people-system: the thinking processes and attitudes.
- The will of a people-system: making corporate choices and decisions.

Body

The "flesh and bones" of a people-system:

- Structures such as buildings
- Policies and procedures such as constitutions
- The ways it portrays itself such as websites
- How members of the people-system interface with one another such as small groups.

The body of a people-system is the expression of the interplay of the spirit, soul, and brain (leadership) of the people-system.

A great mistake is to assume that we can lead by first changing the *body* of a people-system rather than by promoting health and positive change in the *spirit* and *soul* of the people-system.

Pause For Thought

The idea of people-systems might be a completely new concept to you, but you will certainly have experienced their influence.

How have you experienced the influence of people-systems in your life and in your leadership?

When have you seen effective leadership in a people-system?

When have you seen a people-system destroy good leadership?

The Leadership Dilemma

Becoming a healthy leader is one of our greatest responsibilities. Yet being a healthy leader alone does not determine our fruitfulness as a leader. A healthy people-system will often help make an unhealthy leader effective; an unhealthy people-system will often render a healthy leader ineffective. This means that our people-system will determine our leadership effectiveness far more than we realize.

WALK IT OUT

What was the outcome of your action item(s) from the last session?

How will you apply what you have learned this week?

Pray for one another in your leadership responsibilities.

For further information on the topics covered in this session, see the accompanying book, *Freed To Lead*, by Rod Woods, chapter 6.

Setting Your Ministry Free

Nothing takes the wind out of a church's or ministry's sails more than dysfunctional leadership, internal strife, unresolved conflict, and unresolved sin from the past. Freedom In Christ Ministries regularly facilitates retreats for church and ministry leadership teams to resolve these issues.

Leaders report significant breakthroughs, an end to repeating patterns of division and other sins, and a new sense of unity.

The retreats are based on the process outlined in *Setting Your Church Free* or *Extreme Church Makeover* by Neil Anderson and Charles Mylander.

This is a process of establishing the healthy leadership patterns needed to guide a Spirit-led process of renewal and refocusing. During the process leadership teams address corporate sins, spiritual attacks, and destructive corporate mindsets. They finish by putting together a Prayer Action Plan that guides them as they seek to apply what God shows them during the retreat during the following weeks and months.

For further information contact your local Freedom In Christ representative (see page 8).

SESSION 5:

Building Healthy People-Systems

What does a perfect day look like to you?

Read Psalm 37:14–16.

Thank God for how He cares for the poor and needy and how He provides for His people.

WORD

Read

Read Colossians 3:2–17.

- What are the things that we are encouraged to do ourselves?
- What are the things that we are encouraged to allow someone else to do in us or for us?

Understand

- Who wrote this passage?
- To whom is it written?
- What is the main theme of this passage?

Discern

- How does Paul describe the people to whom he is writing?
- What does Paul say to the people to "put on" or "let dwell within" you?
- What does Paul say to the people they should do?
- How should these things be done?
- Why should they be done?

Apply

- How do the traits which we are to "put on" or "let dwell within" become a part of us?
- How do these traits affect you as a leader?
- How do these traits in you affect the group you lead?

Commit

- When is it most difficult to demonstrate the traits described in this passage in your own life?
- What actions might increase your ability to "put on" the traits to which Paul refers?
- What attitudes increase your ability to exercise these traits in your leadership – both your attitudes and the attitudes of those you lead?

Healthy People-Systems

Without healthy leadership, it's impossible for an unhealthy people-system to become healthy.

Leadership is the primary determinant of whether people-systems remain healthy or become even more fruitful.

Three hallmarks of healthy leaders:

1. Having our being grounded in Jesus
2. Genuine humility – a sober, truth-filled view of ourselves and a knowledge of the greatness of God
3. Holy determination – perseverance.

> Pause For Thought
>
> **We've talked a lot about what makes a good leader. Sometimes it's helpful to learn from the opposite example. We can learn what not to do in leadership and discover what can make our leadership ineffective.**
>
> **What makes a bad leader?**
> **What disrupts effective leadership?**
> **How do you know when a people-system is healthy?**

Three characteristics of healthy people-systems:

1. Mutual submission

Submit to one another out of reverence for Christ.
Ephesians 5:21

2. Unity

Behold, how good and pleasant it is when brothers dwell in unity! It is like the precious oil on the head, running down on the beard, on the beard of Aaron, running down on the collar of his robes! It is like the dew of Hermon, which falls on the mountains of Zion! For there the LORD has commanded the blessing, life forevermore.

Psalm 133

I therefore, a prisoner for the Lord, urge you to walk in a manner worthy of the calling to which you have been called, with all humility and gentleness, with patience, bearing with one another in love, eager to maintain the unity of the Spirit in the bond of peace. There is one body and one Spirit – just as you were called to the one hope that belongs to your call – one Lord, one faith, one baptism, one God and Father of all, who is over all and through all and in all.

Ephesians 4:1–6

I appeal to you, brothers, by the name of our Lord Jesus Christ, that all of you agree, and that there be no divisions among you, but that you be united in the same mind and the same judgment.

1 Corinthians 1:10

3. Love

And above all these put on love, which binds everything together in perfect harmony.

Colossians 3:14

Unhealthy People-Systems

Three characteristics of dysfunctional people-systems:

1. Rebelliousness – refusing to co-operate; making demands
2. Factionalism – secrets, gossip and rumours
3. Selfism – a radical sense of selfishness.

Building Healthy People-Systems

The power to influence our people-system towards health flows from *our being*:

- Our own spiritual health – significance, security, and acceptance grounded in Jesus Christ
- Our genuine and authentic commitment to our people – a tangible loving presence in their midst.

In most marriages, the husband and wife commit to one another "in sickness and in health". If we are to have a lasting influence in our people-systems as leaders, we must also commit ourselves to them in sickness and in health.

The Bane Of Leadership – Anxiety

Anxiety: the painful and disturbing unease or apprehension that stems from inappropriate concern about something uncertain.

- Acute anxiety – episodic.
- Chronic anxiety – ongoing, persistent, habitual.

Anxiety In The Bible

> *...for God gave us a spirit not of fear but of power and love and self-control.*
>
> *2 Timothy 1:7*

Fear: "cowardice or failure of nerve that comes from anxiety".

> *Humble yourselves, therefore, under the mighty hand of God so that at the proper time he may exalt you, casting all your anxieties on him, because he cares for you. Be sober-minded; be watchful. Your adversary the devil prowls around like a roaring lion, seeking someone to devour. Resist him, firm in your faith, knowing that the same kinds of suffering are being experienced by your brotherhood throughout the world.*
>
> *1 Peter 5:6–9*

This passage shows a connection between anxiety and the demonic – anxiety makes Christians susceptible to demonic attack.

"Anxiety" can also be translated as "concern" or "care." It describes an emotional state that causes us to attach importance to something. Like anger, it indicates that something needs to be addressed.

Roots Of Anxiety

- Identity and integrity not grounded in Jesus Christ.
- Lost and ungrounded – lacking confidence.
- Overloaded and confused.
- Loss aversion.
- Idolatry (trusting people and things rather than God).
- Not taking appropriate responsibility.

Features Of Anxiety

1. Anxiety is infectious.
2. Anxiety disguises itself.
3. Anxiety distorts everything in a person and a people-system.
4. Anxiety weakens the natural defences of people and people-systems – both become susceptible to the influence of outside forces.
5. Anxiety is resistible.

Anxiety And The Demonic

Anxiety is a spiritual dynamic as well as an emotional dynamic. Demons, including principalities and powers, seek to produce and magnify anxiety in people and people-systems in order to control them. Left unresolved, anxiety will give a foothold for the demonic in any person or people-system.

Recognizing Anxiety

<table>
<tr>
<td>Symptoms Of Anxiety In People

• Loss of imagination
• Inability to reason
• Inability to choose
• Emotionality
• Distorted communication
• Defensiveness
• "Too much" syndrome – too much food, alcohol, TV, etc
• Seeking quick fixes
• Restlessness
• Helplessness</td>
<td>Symptoms Of Anxiety In People-Systems

• Intolerance of pain
• Adjusting to immaturity and irresponsibility
• Preoccupation with comfort and convenience
• Fad issues and cures
• Corporate self-centredness
• Focusing on rights
• Obsession with rules
• Exaggeration
• Vague, ill-defined complaints
• Groupthink</td>
</tr>
<tr>
<td>Chronic Anxiety in People

• Wilfulness
• Self-centredness
• Fault-finding and criticism
• Blame-shifting
• Harmful behaviours</td>
<td>Chronic Anxiety in People-Systems

• Fixate on what they perceive to be the problem
• Gather in factions
• Fixate on peripheral issues such as health and safety
• Develop unrealistic expectations
• Attacking one another personally, especially leaders</td>
</tr>
</table>

Static In Communication

When anxiety is present in a person or a system, it always hinders good communication.

Anxiety Producers In Communication	Anxiety Reducers In Communication
• Anger • Emotionality • Rumours and secrets (even when people don't know about them) • Complaining and grumbling	• Being calm and gentle • Being hopeful • Having transparency and openness • Smiling • Listening actively • Moderating your speech and tone • Sincere praise and thanksgiving • Embracing pain in yourself and others

To the degree that we have unmanaged or unresolved anxiety, we cannot lead effectively. Anxiety in the leader always produces or magnifies anxiety in the people-system.

For further reading on anxiety we recommend *A Failure Of Nerve* by Edwin H. Friedman (Seabury Books, 2007).

Pause For Thought

We often fail to consider how the health of our people-system influences our leadership effectiveness.

Based on what you have learned in this session, how would you evaluate the current health of the people-system you lead?

How have you seen the effects of anxiety in your life, your leadership, or the people-systems you are part of?

What other sicknesses have you seen influence people-systems? How did you overcome those sicknesses?

The Leadership Dilemma

True leadership is the only way we have of resolving chronic anxiety, whether in people or people-systems. Yet true leadership often intensifies anxiety before leading people and people-systems out of anxiety. Things can seem to get much worse before they get better.

With your being grounded in Christ and your doing flowing from your being you *can* lead your people-system to health.

WALK IT OUT

What was the outcome of your action item(s) from the last session?

How will you apply what you have learned this week?

Pray for the health of each people-system represented in your group.

For further information on the topics covered in this session, see the accompanying book, *Freed To Lead*, by Rod Woods, chapters 6 and 9.

SESSION 6:

Overcoming Personal Anxiety

What was your most embarrassing moment?

Read Psalm 37:17–20.

Thank and praise God for how He cares for, protects, and provides for His people during difficult times.

WORD

Read

Read 1 Peter 5:6–11.

Read the passage again and note every promise from God in the passage. Note whether the promises are conditional or unconditional. What might keep us from receiving the promises?

Understand

- Who wrote this passage?
- To whom is this passage written?
- Why was this passage/letter written?

Discern

- What does this passage teach us about the person and nature of God?
- What do you think it means to humble ourselves?

- What are anxieties? What do you think it means to cast all our anxieties on God?
- What do you think it means for the devil to "prowl around like a roaring lion"? What would that look like in practice?
- What would it look like for the devil to "devour" someone?
- What does God promise in verse 10? What do you think each promise means?
- What is the significance of Peter's declaration in verse 11?

Apply

- What is the "proper time" to which Peter refers (verse 6)? How would we recognize it?
- What do you think it means to resist the devil? How might we do this?
- How does knowing that other Christians are experiencing the same kinds of suffering help us to be firm in our faith?
- What characteristics or activities of God mentioned by Peter might comfort and encourage us?
- What is the role or purpose of suffering (verses 9–10) in this passage?
- How have you experienced each of God's promises in verse 10 in your life in the past?
- In light of this passage, what might you expect as a leader – both positively and negatively?

Commit

- What would it look like for you as a leader to cast all your anxieties on God?
- How might you be sober-minded and watchful regarding your leadership?

WATCH

Anxiety in a man's heart weights him down, but a good word makes him glad.

Proverbs 12:25

Therefore do not be anxious about tomorrow, for tomorrow will be anxious for itself. Sufficient for the day is its own trouble.

Matthew 6:34

Do not be anxious about anything, but in everything by prayer and supplication with thanksgiving let your requests be made known to God.

Philippians 4:6

Anxiety Definition

The painful and disturbing

unease or apprehension

that stems from

inappropriate

concern

about something uncertain.

> Concern is a natural emotion. It's an indicator that something is important to you. Not all concern is inappropriate.
>
> Appropriate concern comes from a realistic and truth-filled assessment of the situation.

> Inappropriate concern is habitual, ongoing and unresolved – not based on truth that comes from the Word of God.

Strategies To Resolve Personal Anxiety

> ***Humble yourselves**, therefore, under the mighty hand of God so that at the proper time he may exalt you, **casting all your anxieties on him**, because he cares for you. Be sober-minded; be watchful. Your adversary the devil prowls around like a roaring lion, seeking someone to devour. Resist him, firm in your faith, knowing that the same kinds of suffering are being experienced by your brotherhood throughout the world.*
>
> *1 Peter 5:6–9*

Resolving Anxiety Is A Choice

Do not be anxious about tomorrow.

Matthew 6:34

Do not be anxious about anything.

Philippians 4:6

1. Humble Yourselves

- Let go of our own agenda.
- Let go of wrong goals.

> **Goals and Desires**
>
> Any goal that can be blocked by other people or circumstances that you have no right or ability to control is not a goal that God wants you to have. "Downgrade" it to the category of "desire".

2. Cast Your Anxiety On To God

Through prayer, determine the following:

- What is God's responsibility?
- What is someone else's responsibility?
- What is your responsibility?

Do what you need to do to fulfil your responsibilities

- Forgiveness
- Repentance
- Making amends

Then leave the rest to God.

The Steps To Freedom In Christ by Neil Anderson (see page 30) contains a very practical way of doing this in its "Anxiety Appendix".

Practise Spiritual Disciplines

Rejoice in the Lord always; again I will say, Rejoice.

Let your reasonableness be known to everyone.

The Lord is at hand; do not be anxious about anything, but in everything by prayer and supplication with thanksgiving

let your requests be made known to God [with thanksgiving].

And the peace of God, which surpasses all understanding, will guard your hearts and your minds in Christ Jesus.

Philippians 4:4–7

1. Rejoice in the Lord always.

2. Let your reasonableness be known to everyone.

3. Be obviously generous and magnanimous.

4. Pray – let your requests be known to God.

5. Give thanks.

6. Persevere until the peace of God guards your heart and mind.

If what we perceive does not reflect the truth, what we feel will not reflect reality.

> **Pause For Thought**
>
> Let's practise thanksgiving right now with the "Five-Minute Thanksgiving Challenge". Set a timer for five minutes and then thank God during that time. Don't thank Him for an item more than once.
>
> How difficult was the five-minute thanksgiving challenge for you?
>
> Of the disciplines listed, which is the most difficult for you and why?
>
> What step will you take tomorrow to improve that discipline in your life?

Choose Your Focus

Finally, brothers, whatever is true, whatever is honourable, whatever is just, whatever is pure, whatever is lovely, whatever is commendable, if there is any excellence, if there is anything worthy of praise, think [and keep on thinking] about these things.

What you have learned and received and heard and seen in me – practise these things, and the God of peace will be with you.

Philippians 4:8–9

- What you have learned – godly discipleship.
- What you have received – godly traditions.
- What you have heard – godly teaching.
- What you have seen – first-hand examples of Christian living.

Recognize That Conflict In Leadership Is Inevitable

Conflict is nothing to be frightened of. It is going to happen from time to time.

The question is simply this: how will you handle it?

Choose To Respond Rather Than React

Reactive – acting out of instinct and reflex.

Responsive – acting out of intention and choice, exercising self-control.

Embrace Pain

God uses pain to develop character in us and in the people we lead.

We need to care for those we lead but we are not responsible for their problems. Just as God refuses to step in and do things that are our responsibility, we need to refuse to step in to "rescue" them or "medicate" them by making them feel better when it would be better for them to persevere and become more mature.

Remember The Sabbath

- Take your holidays.
- Take retreats.

Manage Stress

- Know your vulnerabilities

  What are your particular temptations?

  What is the way of escape?
- Rest, eat, and exercise.
- Control your gadgets.

Wait On The Lord

They who wait for the LORD shall renew their strength;

they shall mount up with wings like eagles;

they shall run and not be weary;

they shall walk and not faint.

Isaiah 40:31

Pause For Thought

We've introduced a number of strategies in this session to help resolve and overcome anxiety in our lives as leaders. Consider ways to implement the strategies in your life.

How do you observe the Sabbath?

Which strategy to overcome anxiety resonated with you most strongly?

What will you do about it?

What has been the biggest insight for you from this session?

Key Themes For Personal Growth As Leaders

We have emphasized the need to work on our *being* as leaders because our doing flows from our being. As we go through *Freed To Lead* you will notice that this boils down to a few key themes:

1. Know who you are in Christ.
2. Ruthlessly close any doors you've opened to the enemy through past sin and don't open any more.
3. Renew your mind to the truth of Gods Word (which is how you will be transformed).
4. Work from a place of rest.

The Leadership Dilemma

Anxiety always hides or disguises itself so we can be completely unaware of our own anxiety and how it is influencing our leadership. Anxiety also undermines the self-control and renewing of the mind we need to help us overcome it.

WALK IT OUT

What was the outcome of your action item(s) from the last session?

How will you apply what you have learned this week?

Pray for one another, focusing especially on anything that seems to be causing anxiety in your group.

You will be encouraged to work through *The Steps To Freedom For Leaders* at the end of this course. But if something in this session has prompted you to want to examine the issue of anxiety in you as a leader more closely, you might like to look at Step 3 (pages 151–156) now.

> For further information on the topics covered in this session, see the accompanying book, *Freed To Lead*, by Rod Woods, chapter 10.

SESSION 7:

Overcoming Group Anxiety

What is your strongest personal quality?

Read Psalm 37:21–24.

Pray that your generosity and giving might reflect the generosity and giving of God.

Thank God for the tokens of His generosity in your life.

Read

Read Ephesians 6:10–20 and 2 Timothy 2:24–26.

Read the passages again and mark each word that indicates an adversary to our leadership. What do the marked words suggest about the nature of the battles we face as leaders?

Understand

- Who wrote these passages?
- To whom are these passages written?
- Why were these passages/letters written?

Discern

- What is the purpose of the armour of God?
- What is our ultimate objective in the Ephesians passage (verses 13–14) and in the 2 Timothy passage (verse 26)?
- What is the activity of the devil ("spiritual forces of evil") in the two passages?
- What do you think it means to "pray at all times in the Spirit"?
- What does it look like to be quarrelsome? What is not being quarrelsome according to Paul?
- What is the "snare of the devil"?

Apply

- What does it mean to take a stand and stand firm? How does that relate to leadership?
- Why is it important to keep alert with perseverance?
- We wrestle not against "flesh and blood", but we are to correct "opponents" – clearly meaning people. How do we reconcile the two ideas?
- Why do you think it is so important not to "be quarrelsome", especially as a leader?
- Why does Paul say that God "may perhaps" grant repentance instead of saying that God "will" grant repentance?
- Which comes first: repentance or the knowledge of the truth? Why might this be significant?
- In light of this passage, what might you expect as a leader – both positively and negatively?

Commit

In your leadership, how might you balance the ideas of wrestling not against flesh and blood and correcting your opponents with gentleness?
In light of this passage what might you do as a leader when opposed by people?

Becoming An Anxiety-Resistant Leader

Chronic anxiety has infected the people-systems of society – including churches.

The only way for people-systems to resist and resolve chronic anxiety is to have anxiety-resistant leaders who are totally committed and connected to their people-system.

Remember:

- God gave us a spirit of power and love and self-control (2 Timothy 1:7)
- Put on the whole armour of God (Ephesians 6:11)
- People are not the enemy (Ephesians 6:12)
- Take a stand and then stand firm (Ephesians 6:13–14)

We need to maintain the health of our *being* if we are to become leaders who help people-systems resolve group anxiety.

Five Behaviours Of Anxious People-Systems

1. Reactivity
2. Herding
3. Blame-shifting
4. Quick-fix mentality
5. Leadership abdication.

Reactivity

Reactivity: *a cycle of intense, reflexive reactions between people or groups, "getting stuck" in a negative and sinful way of relating to one another.*

Characteristics Of Reactivity

- Overly intense emotions
- Pessimism
- Violation of legitimate personal boundaries
- Interrupting, speaking over one another, refusing to listen
- Overreaction to perceived hurt, insult, or slight
- Take disagreements too seriously
- Personal attacks rather than dealing with legitimate issues.

Effects Of Reactivity On People-Systems

- A focus on self-preservation and stability
- Defend and justify reactive behaviour
- A loss of resources
- Destructive and demonized.

Overcoming Reactivity

- Exercise self-control
- Give grace to one another
- Identify and evaluate perceptions
- Respond thoughtfully with gentle firmness – take a stand
- Focus on health – both healthy processes and healthy people
- Move in the opposite spirit
    - Forgiveness not bitterness
    - Calm not anger
    - Appreciation not criticism.

> *And the Lord's servant must not be quarrelsome but kind to everyone, able to teach, patiently enduring evil, correcting his opponents with gentleness. God may perhaps grant them repentance leading to a knowledge of the truth, and they may come to their senses and escape from the snare of the devil, after being captured by him to do his will.*
>
> *2 Timothy 2:24–26*

Pause For Thought

Reactivity is one of the most common effects of anxiety in a people-system. Most of us have actually witnessed reactivity at one time or another. Most likely, we didn't realize what was happening.

Describe a time when you have seen two people or groups caught up in reactivity.

What was the outcome?

What could people have done to make the outcome better?

Herding

Herding: *a strong pressure for some kind of idealistic cohesion that does not allow people to take responsibility and act maturely.*

Characteristics Of Herding

- A desire to "just get along for the common good"
- Adapting to the least mature, most dependent or dysfunctional member.

Overcoming Herding

- Focus on the mature people in the people-system.
- Emphasize strengths in people and in the people-system.
- Encourage integrity, maturity, and responsibility.
- Be emotionally open and available.
- Take clear, principled stands on issues but remain connected to people.

Blame-Shifting

Blame-shifting: *a focus on forces that are believed to victimize rather than taking personal responsibility for your own being and doing.*

Overcoming Blame-Shifting

- Reframe the issues in relation to the people-system itself.
- Focus on maturity and mature people in the people-system.
- Review perceptions and expectations.
- Describe challenges and respond to those challenges in terms of the healthy aspects of the people-system.
- Encourage people to take appropriate responsibility for themselves by modelling it for them.

Quick-Fix Mentality

Quick-fix mentality: *a low threshold for pain that causes people to seek symptom relief rather than change and maturity.*

Overcoming Quick-Fix Mentality

- Embrace pain and difficulty.
- Encourage, allow and defend time and space for processes to mature.
- Expose idealistic distortions.
- Establish clear and realistic "signposts" to demonstrate progress.

Leadership Abdication

Leadership abdication: *a "failure of nerve" that inclines leaders to neglect the responsibilities of leadership and capitulate to the above-mentioned behaviours.*

Overcoming Leadership Abdication

- Exercise self-control and steadfastness.
- Seek your own maturity and integrity.
- Walk by the Spirit of God.
- Embrace the responsibilities of leadership.
- Accept the consequences of your decisions.
- Commit to persevere in leadership.
- Put a symbolic stake in the ground.

Leading People-Systems Out Of Anxiety

Effective leaders of people-systems:

- take responsibility for themselves so they become anxiety-resistant leaders
- expect relentless resistance, opposition, and sabotage
- submit fully to God
- seek to shape the mindsets of their people-system with faith, hope, and love
- become "lightning rods" – grounded in Jesus and draining away anxiety.

The Leadership Dilemma

Authentic, healthy, connected leaders are the only hope for resolving anxiety in any people-system. But chronically anxious people-systems will always try to eliminate healthy leaders from the system before anxiety is resolved.

Pause For Thought

We really want to emphasize that you *can* overcome anxiety in your people-system. All people-systems will encounter anxiety from time to time – we can't avoid it. But we don't have to be victims.

How have you seen anxiety at work in the various people-systems that you are part of? What has been the impact?

How have you sought to manage and resolve anxiety in the past? How effective has this been?

Think of one way anxiety is manifesting in your people-system. How will you seek to resolve this anxiety based on what you have learned in this session?

WALK IT OUT

What was the outcome of your action item(s) from the last session?

How will you apply what you have learned this week?

Pray for any anxiety present in one another's people-systems. Pray especially that each one would have wisdom for overcoming this anxiety in the people-system.

Reflect on your own leadership experiences using the leadership timeline on page 18:

- Think about some periods when you have experienced personal anxiety. What else was happening around you? How did it affect your leadership?
- How have you seen group anxiety arise in your leadership context?

You will be encouraged to work through *The Steps To Freedom For Leaders* at the end of this course. But if something in this session has prompted you to want to examine your identity as a leader more closely, you might like to look at Step four (on pages 157–162) now.

For further information on the topics covered in this session, see the accompanying book, *Freed To Lead,* by Rod Woods, chapter 11.

SESSION 8:

Building And Keeping Trust

What quality is most important to you in a friend?

Read Psalm 37:25–28.

Thank God for your physical or spiritual children and the promise that they shall become a blessing.

WORD

Read

Read 1 Corinthians 4:1–5 and 2 Corinthians 3:1–6.

Read the passages again and note all words containing "commend". Then note all words containing "judge". Finally, note all words containing "sufficient". What stands out to you?

Understand

- Who wrote these passages?
- To whom are the passages written?
- Why were these passages/letters written?

Discern

- What is a "steward"? What is the relationship between being a "steward" and being a "servant"?
- What are the mysteries of God to which Paul is referring?
- What does Paul mean by the words "judge" or "judgment"?

- According to Paul, who is – and is not – the one responsible to "judge"? Why would Paul not even judge himself?
- What does it mean to be "sufficient"? Who has made us sufficient? Does this just apply to our "ministry" or does it apply to our lives generally?
- How does the "letter" kill? How does the Spirit give life?

Apply

- As a leader, what is the gift of God that is in you?
- What is the relationship between "faithfulness" and trust?
- What is the basis of our commendation as leaders?
- What is the possible relationship between our commendation as leaders and our trustworthiness as leaders?
- "The letter kills, but the Spirit gives life." How is this true regarding our leadership?
- In light of this passage, what might you expect as a leader – both positively and negatively?

Commit

- How will this passage affect your tendency to judge yourself and your leadership (as well as the leadership of others)?

Trust

This is how one should regard us, as servants of Christ and stewards of the mysteries of God. Moreover, it is required of stewards that they be found trustworthy.

1 Corinthians 4:1–2

> Pause For Thought
>
> **In our hearts we know that trust is important, but perhaps we do not appreciate how important trust really is to our effectiveness as leaders as well as to the health of our people-systems.**
>
> **Who is the person you most trust in your life? Why?**
>
> **Do you consider yourself worthy of trust as a leader? Why or why not?**
>
> **How would you define "trust"?**

Indicators Of A Low Trust People-System

Atmosphere Of Suspicion

- Manipulated or distorted facts
- Spinning the truth
- Withholding information
- Blaming, criticism, accusation
- Secrets and secret meetings.

Atmosphere Of Anxiety

- Unwillingness to take risks
- Mistakes covered up
- Overpromising and underdelivering.

Atmosphere Of Tension And Friction

- Getting personal credit is important
- Open resistance to new ideas and change
- Unrealistic expectations.

Indicators Of A High Trust People-System

Atmosphere Of Openness

- Information is shared openly
- Mistakes are tolerated and encouraged
- Authenticity and vulnerability are demonstrated
- Accountability.

Atmosphere Of Honour

- A focus on others instead of self
- Sharing credit
- Honesty
- Loyalty to those not present
- Collaboration and co-operation.

Atmosphere Of Creativity

- Energy and vitality
- Reduced anxiety
- Enhanced teamwork
- Increased innovation and better execution
- Improved communication.

The Atmosphere Of Trust That God Creates

One of the most significant things you can do as a leader is make sure you yourself have a deep understanding of the grace of God. Then simply come to your people the same way God comes to you.

God:

1. Gives us a huge commission and the means to fulfil it
2. Trusts us to do what He has called us to do
3. Gives us freedom to fail
4. Disciplines us in love
5. Is always available
6. Shows unswerving loyalty even when we are disloyal
7. Is slow to anger and abounding in steadfast love. (Psalm 103:8)

Building Trust

All trust flows from two dynamics: being and doing.

Being (Character)	**Doing** (Competence)
Integrity	Abilities
Motive	Skills
Intent	Tangible track record

Trust: *to place your confidence in the being and doing of another.*

The Trust Equation

If people feel your character (being) is right and you are competent (doing), they will trust you.

QB + QD = C

Quality of *Being* + Quality of *Doing* = Amount of *Confidence*

The Apostle Paul On Building Trust

Are we beginning to commend ourselves again? Or do we need, as some do, letters of recommendation to you, or from you? You yourselves are our letter of recommendation, written on our hearts, to be known and read by all. And you show that you are a letter from Christ delivered by us, written not with ink but with the Spirit of the living God, not on tablets of stone but on tablets of human hearts.

2 Corinthians 3:1–3

Such is the confidence that we have through Christ towards God. Not that we are sufficient in ourselves to claim anything as coming from us, but our sufficiency is from God, who has made us competent to be ministers of a new covenant, not of the letter but of the Spirit. For the letter kills, but the Spirit gives life.

2 Corinthians 3:4–5

What we are is known to God, and I hope it is known also to your conscience. We are not commending ourselves to you again but giving you cause to boast about us, so that you may be able to answer those who boast about outward appearance and not about what is in the heart.

2 Corinthians 5:11–12

Trust-Building Behaviours Of Being (Character)

Speak the truth in love

Rather, speaking the truth in love, we are to grow up in every way into him who is the head, into Christ, from whom the whole body, joined and held together by every joint with which it is equipped, when each part is working properly, makes the body grow so that it builds itself up in love.

Ephesians 4:15–16

Show respect and honour

Pay to all what is owed to them: taxes to whom taxes are owed, revenue to whom revenue is owed, respect to whom respect is owed, honour to whom honour is owed.

Romans 13:7

Model transparency

But above all, my brothers, do not swear, either by heaven or by earth or by any other oath, but let your "yes" be yes and your "no" be no, so that you may not fall under condemnation.

James 5:12

Right wrongs

So if you are offering your gift at the altar and there remember that your brother has something against you, leave your gift there before the altar and go. First be reconciled to your brother, and then come and offer your gift. Come to terms quickly with your accuser while you are going with him to court, lest your accuser hand you over to the judge, and the judge to the guard, and you be put in prison.

Matthew 5:23–25

Show loyalty

Many a man proclaims his own steadfast love, but a faithful man who can find?

Proverbs 20:6

Pay attention to others

Let each of you look not only to his own interests, but also to the interests of others.

Philippians 2:4

Exercise self-control

It is not good to eat much honey, nor is it glorious to seek one's own glory. A man without self-control is like a city broken into and left without walls.

Proverbs 25:27–28

Express gratitude

Let there be no filthiness nor foolish talk nor crude joking, which are out of place, but instead let there be thanksgiving.

Ephesians 5:4

Give grace

Be kind to one another, tender-hearted, forgiving one another, as God in Christ forgave you.

Ephesians 4:32

Trust-Building Behaviours Of Doing (Competence)

Deliver results – don't make excuses

Keep your conduct among the Gentiles honourable, so that when they speak against you as evildoers, they may see your good deeds and glorify God on the day of visitation.

1 Peter 2:12

Get better – continually improve on what you do

Give instruction to a wise man, and he will be still wiser; teach a righteous man, and he will increase in learning.

Proverbs 9:9

Confront reality

And Samuel came to Saul, and Saul said to him, "Blessed be you to the LORD. I have performed the commandment of the LORD." And Samuel said, "What then is this bleating of the sheep in my ears and the lowing of the oxen that I hear?" Saul said, "They have brought them from the Amalekites, for the people spared the best of the sheep and of the oxen to sacrifice to the LORD your God, and the rest we have devoted to destruction."

1 Samuel 15:13–15

Clarify expectations

So I thought it necessary to urge the brothers to go on ahead to you and arrange in advance for the gift you have promised, so that it may be ready as a willing gift, not as an exaction. The point is this: whoever sows sparingly will also reap sparingly, and whoever sows bountifully will also reap bountifully. Each one must give as he has decided in his heart, not reluctantly or under compulsion, for God loves a cheerful giver.

2 Corinthians 9:5–7

Practise accountability

So then each of us will give an account of himself to God.

Romans 14:12

Listen actively

Know this, my beloved brothers: let every person be quick to hear, slow to speak, slow to anger; for the anger of man does not produce the righteousness of God.

James 1:19–20

Keep commitments

O LORD, who shall sojourn in your tent? Who shall dwell on your holy hill? … [he] who swears to his own hurt and does not change;

Psalm 15:1 and 4b

Extend trust to others

And some of the men of Benjamin and Judah came to the stronghold to David. David went out to meet them and said to them, "If you have come to me in friendship to help me, my heart will be joined to you; but if to betray me to my adversaries, although there is no wrong in my hands, then may the God of our fathers see and rebuke you." Then the Spirit clothed Amasai, chief of the thirty, and he said, "We are yours, O David, and with you, O son of Jesse! Peace, peace to you, and peace to your helpers! For your God helps you." Then David received them and made them officers of his troops.

1 Chronicles 12:16–18

Meet the needs of followers

Now in these days when the disciples were increasing in number, a complaint by the Hellenists arose against the Hebrews because their widows were being neglected in the daily distribution. And the twelve summoned the full number of the disciples and said, "It is not right that we should give up preaching the word of God to serve tables. Therefore, brothers, pick out from among you seven men of good repute, full of the Spirit and of wisdom, whom we will appoint to this duty. But we will devote ourselves to prayer and to the ministry of the word." And what they said pleased the whole gathering, and they chose Stephen, a man full of faith and of the Holy Spirit, and Philip, and Prochorus, and Nicanor, and Timon, and Parmenas, and Nicolaus, a proselyte of Antioch. These they set before the apostles, and they prayed and laid their hands on them.

Acts 6:1–6

Losing And Regaining Trust

Trust takes time to build but can be lost in an instant.

The quickest way to destroy trust is for your behaviour to cause people to doubt your being – your integrity, your goodwill. That will happen if you violate a trust-building behaviour of being.

The quickest way to increase trust is through your doing – your actions, your abilities, your competence.

To rebuild trust you must:

- Stop violating trust-building behaviours of being
- Intentionally practise trust-building behaviours of doing.

The Leadership Dilemma

People-systems can't function without trust. But they are increasingly prone to anxiety which degrades trust. Increasingly society itself is a low-trust environment with people actively trying to destroy trust in leaders. The end result is that there is a corrosive pessimism towards leaders and people-systems.

Pause For Thought

Hopefully this session has helped you understand some ways we can increase trust in ourselves as leaders.

How have you experienced the negative effects of the lack of trust in a person or people-system?

How have you experienced the benefits of trust?

Based on what you have learned in this session, what one or two things could you do to improve your competence and credibility as a leader so that people might trust you more?

WALK IT OUT

What was the outcome of your action item(s) from the last session?

How will you apply what you have learned this week?

Pray for one another, focusing on trust-building behaviours that each person would like to adopt or improve in their leadership.

For further information on the topics covered in this session, see the accompanying book, *Freed To Lead,* by Rod Woods, chapter 13.

SESSION 9:

Overcoming Personal Pitfalls

Why did you choose your profession or leadership position?

Read Psalm 37:29–31.

Surrender yourselves to God afresh and ask God to put His will in your heart.

Read

Read 1 Corinthians 10:6–13.

What are the Old Testament stories to which Paul is referring?

Understand

- Who wrote this passage?
- To whom is this passage written?
- Why was this passage/letter written?

Discern

- What does it mean to "desire evil"? What is the relationship between this and "temptation"?
- What does it mean to put Christ to the test?
- Why does Paul give the warning of verse 12? What does it mean?
- What are the promises in verse 13?

Apply

- What are some common “idols” leaders might have?
- When are we most likely to “grumble” as leaders? What effect does this have on our leadership?
- How do you feel about the fact that you will not face an uncommon temptation (verse 13)?
- Why does Paul suggest that we have to “endure” temptation (verse 13)?
- What is the “way of escape”? When is it easiest to escape temptation?

Commit

- What temptations have you been able to resist or overcome as a leader? How have you seen God’s faithfulness in this?
- What “instruction” (verse 11) from this passage will you apply to your leadership?

WATCH

> **Pause For Thought**
>
> Remember: having struggles and difficulties as a leader does not mean you are not a good leader.
>
> What are the greatest challenges you face personally as a leader?
> What are the greatest temptations you face personally as a leader?

Types Of Personal Leadership Pitfall

Pitfalls: *hidden or unexpected dangers or difficulties.*

1. Temptation
2. Self-centredness
3. Emotional
4. Communication
5. Exhaustion.

Temptation Pitfalls

Temptations pitfalls: *strong temptations to find significance, security, and acceptance outside of God.*

Money – including all the financial and material resources God has provided

- Poor personal and organisational money management – debt, bill paying, giving.
- Attitudes about money – greed, covetousness, envy.

Sex

- Wrong ways of thinking – fantasy, daydreaming, lust.
- Wrong actions – pornography, immorality, adultery.
- Wrong situations –"one to one" with no code of practice.

Power

- Desire for control, position or titles, respect.
- Manipulation and dominance.

Avoiding Temptation Pitfalls

- Lead from your identity in Christ – you are significant, secure, and accepted.
- Guard your heart and mind.
- Take the way of escape.

  1 Corinthians 10:13 promises a way of escape from *every* temptation. Where is it? Right at the start of the process, when the tempting thought first comes into your mind.

Paul says in Romans 6 that the power of sin is broken in your life if you are a Christian. That is the truth whether it *feels* true or not.

Self-Centredness Pitfalls

Self-centredness pitfalls: *thinking of leadership from a self-centred perspective.*

Messiah – thinking that you are the saviour of your system or situation

- Arrogance
- Pride
- Selfish ambition
- Manipulation.

A messiah pitfall arises from trying to find significance in leadership rather than in Jesus.

Martyr – thinking that your system requires your suffering or sacrifice to achieve good outcomes

- Control
- Manipulation through shame or guilt
- Avoidance.

A martyr pitfall arises from trying to find acceptance in leadership rather than in Jesus.

Hermit – feeling overwhelmed by stress, conflict, problems or responsibilities

- Retreat
- Narrow focus
- Ignore people
- Deny reality
- Passivity and acquiescence
- Cowardice – a failure of nerve.

A hermit pitfall arises from trying to find security in leadership rather than in Jesus.

Emotional Pitfalls

Emotional pitfalls: *following or being controlled by strong, negative emotions.*

Bitterness – failing to forgive others

- Physical problems such as ulcers
- Disrupted and destroyed relationships
- Malice
- Hatred.

Anger – having a blocked goal

- Resentment
- Frustration
- Impatience
- Irritation
- Rage.

Defensiveness – seeking to protect and justify yourself, taking offence

- Oversensitive
- Thin-skinned
- Prickly
- Overly emotional.

Christian leaders never need to defend themselves. If you are wrong, you don't have a defence. If you are right, you don't need a defence because God Himself will defend you.

Communication Pitfalls

Communication pitfalls: *failing to recognize common aspects of communication which can be mistaken as attack or rebellion.*

- Communication engages emotions and is not just an intellectual process
- Be aware of the effects of distance
- Pursuit behaviours such as criticizing and rescuing often indicate a person's desire to engage in communication yet they tend to turn the other person away.

Avoiding Communication Pitfalls

- Engage humour in communication
- Use "close" communication – face-to-face is best – for difficult subjects
- Allow yourself to be "caught" by those engaging in pursuit behaviours:
    - Stop what you are doing and be emotionally open
    - Listen actively
    - Do not assume rebellion or personal attack.

Exhaustion Pitfalls

Exhaustion pitfalls: *failing to rest and recharge our spiritual, emotional, and relational "batteries".*

Blowout – falling into serious sin because of physical, emotional, mental, and spiritual exhaustion

- Sexual Immorality
- "Too much" syndrome
- Sudden sickness or major health issues.

Bankruptcy – the point at which we run out of spiritual, mental, and emotional reserves and insights

- Loss of creativity
- Loss of vitality
- "Recycling" of insights, messages and teachings.

Burnout – a long-term physical, emotional, mental, and spiritual exhaustion

- Overwhelmed
- Helpless
- Hopeless
- Cynical
- Resentful.

Avoiding Exhaustion Pitfalls

"Abide in me, and I in you. As the branch cannot bear fruit by itself, unless it abides in the vine, neither can you, unless you abide in me."

John 15:4

- We get tired because we want to bear fruit.
- Jesus wants us to bear fruit even more than we do ourselves.
- His command, however, was not to bear fruit but to abide in Him.
- We will bear fruit only if we are connected to Jesus, working from a place of internal rest.

*So then, there remains a Sabbath rest for the people of God, for whoever has entered God's rest has also rested from his works as God did from his. Let us therefore **strive** to enter that rest, so that no one may fall by the same sort of disobedience.*

Hebrews 4:9–11

- Prioritize prayer and Bible reading.
- Take time out to seek God and His will for your life.
- Rest.

Avoiding Personal Pitfalls

- Use *The Steps To Freedom In Christ* regularly (see page 30).
- Practise accountability, vulnerability, honesty, humility.
- Practise lifelong learning – take retreats, read books, listen to lectures.
- Remind yourself how damaging pitfalls are personally and to your leadership.

Put on the Lord Jesus Christ, and make no provision for the flesh, to gratify its desires.

Romans 13:14

> **Pause For Thought**
>
> This pause for thought encourages you to get a little vulnerable with one another.
>
> Which "pit" have you fallen into already?
> What steps will you take to get out of it?
> Which "pit" are you closest to falling into at this moment?
> What steps will you take to avoid falling in?

The Leadership Dilemma

We have everything we need in Christ to avoid these pitfalls, but even so, if we are not very careful, we will tend to keep falling into them.

REMINDER! Key Themes For Personal Growth As Leaders

1. Know who you are in Christ.
2. Ruthlessly close any doors you've opened to the enemy through past sin and don't open any more.
3. Renew your mind to the truth of God's Word (which is how you will be transformed).
4. Work from a place of rest.

WALK IT OUT

What was the outcome of your action item(s) from the last session?

How will you apply what you have learned this week?

Pray for one another in the personal pitfalls that you might be facing.

You will be encouraged to work through *The Steps To Freedom For Leaders* at the end of this course. But if something in this session has prompted you to want to examine the area of pitfalls in your personal life you might like to look at Steps 5 and 6 (pages 163–179) now.

For further information on the topics covered in this session, see the accompanying book, *Freed To Lead*, by Rod Woods, chapters 12 and 14.

Words From An Older Leader To A Younger Leader

You then, my child, be strengthened by the grace that is in Christ Jesus, and what you have heard from me in the presence of many witnesses entrust to faithful men who will be able to teach others also. Share in suffering as a good soldier of Christ Jesus. No soldier gets entangled in civilian pursuits, since his aim is to please the one who enlisted him. An athlete is not crowned unless he competes according to the rules. It is the hard-working farmer who ought to have the first share of the crops. Think over what I say, for the Lord will give you understanding in everything.

2 Timothy 2:1–7

SESSION 10:

Overcoming Group Pitfalls

What famous person would you like to have a meal with? And what is the first question you'd want to ask that person?

Read Psalm 37:32–36.

Surrender any difficult situations or relationships you have to God, asking for His deliverance.

Thank God that He will not abandon you, that He will be your defender.

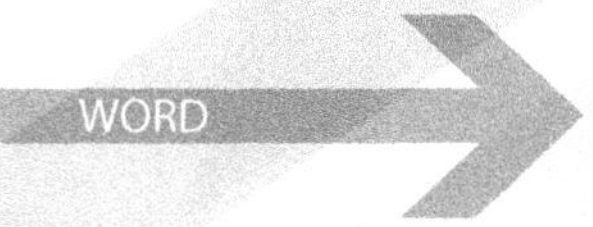

Read

Read 2 Corinthians 2:1–11.

Read the passage again. Note all the words to do with "pain". What strikes you about the results?

Understand

- Who wrote this passage?
- To whom is this passage written?
- Why was this passage/letter written?

Discern

- According to Paul, who or what has caused pain?
- What is the connection between pain and love in verse 4?
- What are the godly Christian responses to pain and those who cause us pain in this passage?

Apply

- What role does "pain" play in leadership?
- How and when might leaders justly cause pain in others?
- How might Satan outwit us if we do not respond to pain appropriately?
- What are some of the "designs" or "schemes" of Satan that might emerge in painful situations?
- According to this passage, what are some possible consequences of sinful behaviour to a people-system?
- Why is forgiveness so important to Paul in this passage?
- In light of this passage, what might you expect as a leader – both positively and negatively?

Commit

In your leadership, when have you experienced pain? When might you have caused pain? How did you respond? How might you respond differently now?

How have you seen Satan's schemes at work in the painful situations you've faced? What strategies might you employ to overcome those schemes?

Group Pitfalls

Group pitfalls: *a set of predictable (but not inevitable) reactions within your people-system in response to* ***effective*** *leadership.*

- Effective leadership will *always* trigger a number of reactions.
- These reactions indicate that our leadership is effective!
- It's not the reaction itself that is the pitfall but our potential wrong response to it.

Dilemmas Not Problems

Problems – issues that can be solved and resolved.

Dilemmas – issues that by their nature cannot be solved, only managed.

Group pitfalls are *dilemmas* and require time and effort to work through.

Four Common Group Pitfalls

1. Selfishness
2. Sabotage
3. Strife
4. Suffering.

Selfishness

Selfishness: *an inappropriate focus on self.*

Symptoms of selfishness:

- Self-centred
- Self-seeking
- Self-referential
- Immaturity – unwillingness or inability to take responsibility for one's mind, will and emotions. Often mistaken for rebellion.

To help your people-system avoid the pitfall of selfishness:

- Model healthy self-giving
- Promote maturity by being mature – take responsibility
- Focus on healthy and mature people in the system without giving in to selfishness.

Sabotage

Sabotage: *seeking to destroy, damage, obstruct, or hinder leaders or change.*

Sources of sabotage:

- Personal or political advantage
- Changing relationships and jealousy
- Fleshly attitudes
- Pride
- Demonically inspired.

Common ways that sabotage presents itself:

- Spreading discontent
- Magnifying the potential loss of doing something
- Misrepresenting a leader or a decision
- Passive aggressive behaviour
- Changing your mind after the group has made a decision
- Putting in extra conditions on an agreement late in negotiations or even after negotiations have been completed
- Agreeing publicly while undermining something privately
- Spreading gossip and rumours
- Bullying and intimidation.

To help your people-system avoid the pitfall of sabotage:

- Respond calmly, peacefully, and intentionally
- Focus on building healthy people and healthy processes.

Strife

Strife: *friction and conflict in the people-system; problems within interpersonal relationships.*

Symptoms of strife:

- Reactivity
- Arguments
- Conflicts of will
- Criticism
- Personal attacks.

Ineffective actions when facing strife:

- Explaining or justifying your position
- Defending yourself
- Withdrawing from the conflict and refusing to engage
- Blaming
- Placating or appeasing
- Bargaining.

To help your people-system avoid the pitfall of strife:

- Ensure that you are grounded in Jesus Christ
- Encourage people to work through strife with love, mercy, and grace
- Model appropriate responses to strife.

Suffering

Suffering: *experiencing something that you perceive to be negative or unpleasant.*

Your willingness and ability to embrace suffering will determine the willingness and ability of the people-system you lead to embrace suffering.

Overcoming Group Pitfalls

- Lead from your identity
- Gain fresh perspective
- Welcome conflict as normal and healthy for growth
- Embrace suffering
- Resist idealistic distortions and expectations.

> Pause For Thought
>
> **Most people tend to assume that we face group pitfalls because we're not leading well rather than because of *effective* leadership.**
>
> **Does it surprise you to learn that group pitfalls are the result of healthy leadership? Why or why not?**
>
> **Which group pitfalls have you seen or experienced personally? What has been the effect on the people-system?**
>
> **Have you ever sabotaged something? What would have been a healthier response?**

Leadership Delusions

Delusion: *a false belief or impression we maintain even when it is contradicted by reality.*

Four Leadership Delusions

1. Expertise
2. Empathy
3. Togetherness
4. Position.

The Delusion Of Expertise

The delusion of expertise: *a false belief that maintains that the right knowledge or technique will make us effective leaders.*

The Delusion Of Empathy

The delusion of empathy: *a false belief that maintains that understanding and sensitivity alone will make us effective leaders. It also maintains that we can overcome inappropriate, unhealthy or destructive behaviour with reason, fairness, and sensitivity.*

The Delusion Of Togetherness

The delusion of togetherness: *a false belief that promoting or maintaining consensus will make us effective leaders.*

Togetherness is sometimes mistaken for unity.

The Delusion Of Position

The delusion of position: *a false belief that position, title, or power will make us effective leaders.*

Dispelling Delusions

- Expose the faulty thinking associated with these delusions.
- Lead from your identity in Christ.
- Hold everything loosely – except Jesus.

> Pause For Thought
>
> When thinking about leadership delusions, it's easy for us to get caught up in an either/or mentality. Either things like expertise and empathy are good, or they are bad. However, there's nothing wrong with expertise, empathy, a little togetherness, or having a position of leadership. The delusion is that any of these things in and of themselves will help us lead more effectively. In other words, these are not leadership strategies.
>
> Which delusion have you succumbed to in the past?
>
> What steps will you take to dispel that delusion?
>
> How have you seen others get wrapped up in one or more of the delusions?

The Leadership Dilemma

We call these dilemmas "group pitfalls", but our *being* and *doing* as leaders will determine more than anything else whether our people-systems get stuck in them.

> *For this reason I remind you to fan into flame the gift of God, which is in you through the laying on of my hands, for God gave us a spirit not of fear [or cowardice] but of power and love and self-control.*
>
> *2 Timothy 1:6–7*

WALK IT OUT

What was the outcome of your action item(s) from the last session?

How will you apply what you have learned this week?

Pray for one another to have the courage to respond to any group pitfalls in healthy, responsible ways.

Bless one another in your leadership roles and responsibilities.

For further information on the topics covered in this session, see the accompanying book, *Freed To Lead*, by Rod Woods, chapters 15 and 16.

Step 7 Introduction

Transforming Leadership

These notes accompany the introduction to Step Seven of *The Steps To Freedom For Leaders.*

> *Now I rejoice in my sufferings for your sake, and in my flesh I am filling up what is lacking in Christ's afflictions for the sake of his body, that is, the church, of which I became a minister according to the stewardship from God that was given to me for you, to make the word of God fully known, the mystery hidden for ages and generations but now revealed to his saints. To them God chose to make known how great among the Gentiles are the riches of the glory of this mystery, which is Christ in you, the hope of glory. Him we proclaim, warning everyone and teaching everyone with all wisdom, that we may present everyone mature in Christ. For this I toil, struggling with all his energy that he powerfully works within me.*
> *Colossians 1:24–29*

WATCH

Because Christ Is In Us

We May Become Authentically Ourselves As Leaders

We Have Real Hope

- Our leadership will bring glory to God.
- Our leadership will change lives.
- Our leadership will show Jesus Christ to the world.

We Can Develop Abilities To Boost Our Growth And Effectiveness

1. Know ourselves

We need to give up trying to be someone or something other than who we are.

2. Control ourselves

Self-control is the only biblical form of control.

3. Communicate ourselves

Vulnerability indicates strength: only a strong person will have the courage and ability to become vulnerable.

We Can Transform Our Leadership Through:

1. **Love** – a zealous, self-giving commitment to others for their benefit.

2. **Faith** – choosing to trust and act, often beyond our natural abilities, based on true knowledge of God and His ways. It is founded in relationship through Jesus Christ in the power of the Holy Spirit.

3. **Embracing the cross:**
    - Offering up our reputation and good name
    - Allowing people to revile us and say all manner of evil against us falsely
    - Being excluded and rejected
    - Laying down our "weapons"
    - Accepting the pain of leadership.

4. **Perseverance and endurance**
    - Perseverance – steadfastness in doing something despite difficulty or delay
    - Endurance – bearing up under something that is difficult or unpleasant without giving way.

"The man who can drive himself further once the effort gets painful is the man who will win." (Roger Bannister)

5. **Perspective** – our reference point from which we view our circumstances.

For further information on the topics covered in this session, see the accompanying book, *Freed To Lead*, by Rod Woods, chapter 17.

The Steps To Freedom For Leaders

Introduction

The Steps To Freedom In Christ by Neil T. Anderson is a resource used around the world to help Christians resolve personal and spiritual issues. Based on his books *Victory Over The Darkness* and *The Bondage Breaker*, and founded on the teaching in the Freedom In Christ Discipleship Course, the "Steps" have become an essential discipleship tool for many churches around the world. Churches use the Steps in a variety of ways: in corporate settings, where people pray through the Steps personally as part of a large-group process; in personal settings, where people pray through the Steps with an encourager and a prayer partner; and in individual settings, where people pray through the Steps or use portions of the Steps as part of their personal discipleship. For many churches the Steps are a fundamental part of their ministry, serving as a doorway into church membership or ministry.

The Steps To Freedom For Leaders is a resource focused on the personal and spiritual issues common to people in leadership, be it leadership in the marketplace, leadership in the church, or leadership in the home and community. This resource will enable you to identify and resolve personal and spiritual issues that can weaken, undermine, or even destroy your leadership. In some cases, these issues have become so entwined with our understanding of leadership that we do not even realize that what we are doing is actually preventing us from being the leaders God desires.

How To Use The Leadership Steps

You may use *The Steps To Freedom For Leaders* in the same ways as you can use the original Steps To Freedom: group settings; personal settings; and individual settings. As with the original Steps, we most strongly recommend using the Leadership Steps in a personal setting with an encourager and a prayer partner. Alternatively, two leaders praying through *The Steps To Freedom For Leaders* together would prove very effective.

However you choose to work through the Leadership Steps, it is essential to give yourself time for reflection as you go through the prayer process. Make notes about the various things you sense that God is showing you about yourself and your leadership. Ideas and strategies may come to your mind regarding your present leadership context. Write these ideas down immediately so that they do not distract you from listening to God for how He is calling you to change and grow as a leader.

In order to receive the maximum benefit from using *The Steps To Freedom For Leaders*, we recommend the following:

- Participating in the Freedom In Christ Discipleship Course, reading the four accompanying *Discipleship Series* books by Steve Goss or reading *Victory Over The Darkness* and *The Bondage Breaker* by Neil T. Anderson
- Engaging in *The Steps To Freedom In Christ* in a personal setting
- Familiarity with the "Truth About My Father God" exercise in Step Two of *The Steps To Freedom In Christ*
- Familiarity with the "Stronghold-Busting" exercise taught in the Freedom In Christ Discipleship Course
- Integrating the discipleship truths from the above fully into your life in an ongoing way
- Participating in the *Freed To Lead* course or reading the *Freed To Lead* book by Rod Woods.

In addition to the above, we would also recommend *The Grace Course* from Freedom In Christ Ministries, a course designed to help people overcome common issues regarding grace and legalism. Such legalism is one of the most destructive forces in the life of a leader – just consider the Pharisees in Jesus' day.

Discipleship For Leaders

As with the general Steps, *The Steps To Freedom For Leaders* provide a number of discipleship resources that may be used outside the overall Leadership Steps process to keep your leadership free in Christ and healthy. For example, we would encourage the use of Step 2 (Forgiveness) on a regular basis to ensure that you are forgiving those who wound you in your leadership context. By so doing, you will overcome the unforgiveness and bitterness issues that have destroyed or seriously damaged many leaders. You could use Step 3 (Anxiety and Reactivity) to help your team work together more smoothly and overcome the anxiety in the face of change that often undermines a team's creativity.

As with *The Steps to Freedom In Christ,* we encourage you to use *The Steps To Freedom for Leaders* annually as scheduled maintenance for your leadership.

However you may use *The Steps To Freedom For Leaders,* we pray that God will richly bless your leadership wherever He has called you. We pray that your exercise of leadership will result in praise and glory to our Lord and Saviour, Jesus Christ.

Opening Prayer And Declaration

Before you begin with the opening prayer and declaration, spend a few minutes reflecting on the following questions (or discussing them with your encourager if you are doing this in a personal setting):

- Who is the most influential leader in your life?
- What qualities do you admire most in a leader?
- What qualities most annoy you in a leader?
- What do you remember most about the leadership qualities of your parents?
- Do you see yourself as a leader? Why or why not?
- Do you see yourself as a good leader? Why or why not?
- What talents, skills, knowledge, and spiritual gifts do you have that you use regularly in your leadership?
- What qualities of Jesus' leadership would you like to see grow in your own leadership?
- How would you like to be remembered as a leader ten years from now?
- What is the greatest legacy that you would like to leave as a leader?

If you have a journal, you may want to make notes about your responses to these questions for review each time you work through *The Steps to Freedom For Leaders.*

Opening Prayer

Dear Heavenly Father, I acknowledge You as the one true living God, existing as the Father, Son and Holy Spirit, and the only Lord of my life. I choose to surrender myself fully to You, so that I may become the leader You have created me to be. I give thanks to You that you have reconciled me to Yourself by grace through faith in Your Son, Jesus Christ. I pray that You, the God of our Lord Jesus Christ, the Father of glory, may give me the Spirit of wisdom and of revelation in the knowledge of Jesus. I pray that I may have the eyes of my heart enlightened, so that I may know what is the hope to which You have called me and what are the riches of Your glorious inheritance in the saints. I pray that I may know the immeasurable greatness of Your power towards us who believe, according to the working of Your great might that You worked in Christ when You raised Him from the dead and seated Him at Your right hand in the heavenly places (Ephesians 1:16–20). I want to know and choose to do Your will in the leadership to which You have called me. To that end, I welcome Your Holy Spirit and Your people to lead me in this process. I choose to co-operate with You fully to the glory of my Lord and Saviour, Jesus Christ. Amen.

Declaration

In the name of Jesus Christ, as one sealed by the Spirit of God, I declare that I submit fully to God and resist the devil (James 4:7). I command Satan and all evil spirits to release me and have no influence over me so that I can know and do God's will. I exalt the living Lord Jesus Christ as the One who died on the cross and rose bodily from the dead, who is now seated far above all rule and authority and power and dominion, and above every name that is named, not only in this age but also in the one to come. This Jesus has all things under His feet and is the head over all things for the benefit of the Church, which is His body, the fullness of Him who fills all in all, and of which I am part (Ephesians 1:21–23). I declare that I, ________________(name), belong to Christ and the evil one cannot touch me (1 John 5:18). I declare that I surrender myself fully – my hopes, dreams and leadership – to God the Father, through Jesus Christ the Son, and in the power of the Holy Spirit. Amen.

Step One: Embracing Our Identity In Christ, Not Leadership

The purpose of this Step is to help discern ways in which you have sought identity, significance, security, or acceptance in leadership roles, positions and titles rather than in Jesus Christ.

To the degree that we try to find our sense of significance, security, acceptance, or identity in our leadership, our leadership is likely to be distorted or dysfunctional. To the degree that we find all these things in Jesus, we will discover true freedom to lead as the people God has created us to be.

You are not free to lead if you are finding your identity in your role as a leader, or if you are basing your acceptance on the approval of others, hoping for job security, or finding your significance in what you do as a leader.

If you could no longer function as a leader or serve in your current leadership capacity, would you still be the same person, having the same sense of acceptance, security, and significance?

Use Part 1 below to help you determine the degree to which you have found your significance, security, acceptance, or identity in leadership.

Part 1 – Discerning Wrongful Identity In Leadership

Dear Heavenly Father,

I thank You that by Your grace through faith in Your Son Jesus Christ I have become your chosen child, holy and precious to You. I thank you that in Christ I know that I am significant, secure, and accepted. However, I confess that I have not always chosen to believe that my identity was fully in Christ. I have sought significance, security, and acceptance through my leadership. I ask that Your Holy Spirit reveal to my mind all the ways that I have sinned against You in this regard, so that I might repent. In Jesus' name, I pray. Amen.

Consider the following four lists. Rate each statement in them on a scale of 1 to 5, with 1 being something that is not at all true for you and 5 being something that is very true for you.

Write the total at the base of each section.

Discerning whether we have sought our identity in leadership:

Identity is more than a label. It speaks to the essence of who we are and why we are here. When we begin our journey on earth, the world seems to revolve around us. Inevitably flesh patterns develop over time until we discover who we are in Christ and learn to centre our life around Christ. Such flesh patterns will hinder our ability to lead.

_ I have trouble imagining my life without my leadership responsibilities.
_ I often feel that my "world" revolves around my leadership role.
_ I often take my electronic gadgets on holiday with me so that I can keep up with my leadership responsibilities.
_ I often struggle to stop thinking about my work/leadership role, even when I have a day off or a holiday.
_ All my hobbies and leisure activities tend to relate to my leadership role.
_ I feel that my leadership role is the most significant and meaningful part of my life.
_ My spouse, children, or friends often complain that I spend too much time in my leadership role (or at work).
_ I feel proud to have attained the leadership position I have
_ I deeply relish all the benefits of the leadership position I have attained and would find it very difficult to lose them.
_ When I am talking with people, the first thing I tend to talk about is something to do with my leadership role or responsibilities.
_ **Total**

Discerning whether we have sought our significance in leadership:

What is forgotten in time is of little significance. What is remembered for eternity has the greatest significance. Believing we are insignificant or that our ministries are insignificant will cripple our leadership as will try to find our significance in leadership roles.

- _ I feel that if I did not do the work myself then everything would fall apart.
- _ My leadership role or position gives me a sense that I have a place in this world.
- _ I am a very important part of my organization, perhaps the key to its success.
- _ I focus a lot on the number of people who attend my event, or the publicity it receives.
- _ How much money I make shows the value of my leadership. (Or: How much money I could be making if I were in another field shows the value of my leadership.)
- _ I enjoy telling people the number of emails that I receive each day, the number of people I supervise, or how important my responsibilities are.
- _ I feel hurt or upset when I do not get the credit that I deserve.
- _ I pay much attention to – or draw others' attention to – the number of titles and degrees I have.
- _ I find it difficult to rest because people really need my help or input.
- _ My leadership role helps me feel good about myself.
- _ **Total**

Discerning whether we have sought our security in leadership:

Security relates to eternal rather than temporal matters, which we have no right or ability to control. Insecure leaders will try to manipulate people and events that they believe will offer them some sense of security.

- _ I'm not sure what I would do in my life if I could not continue in my current leadership role or position.
- _ I often feel that I must remain in control of the situation.
- _ When people criticize me, I often find myself getting very defensive.
- _ All my friends and social circles seem to revolve around my leadership role.
- _ If someone were to wrong me at work or in my leadership capacity, I would quickly seek redress through appropriate channels.
- _ As a leader, it is important for me to remain in charge of situations.

_ I often find myself reminding people how busy I am.
_ I feel competitive or jealous when others seem to do well at the same things I do.
_ I feel threatened when I am with others who seem to be more successful than I am.
_ I spend a lot of time thinking about how much I am paid for my leadership role.
_ **Total**

Discerning whether we have sought our acceptance in leadership:

Acceptance by God is more than being tolerated. It means that we are fully forgiven, adopted as a child of God, made a new creation in Christ, and welcomed as a valuable member into the family of God. Knowing this is essential for leaders, who are likely to receive more criticism and rejection than followers.

_ I struggle to say "no" to new responsibilities.
_ I find it difficult to share my personal struggles with others in my leadership sphere or with the people I lead.
_ As a leader, I feel it is very important for me to be liked by those around me.
_ I conceal my thoughts and feelings because if others see the "real me" they would not want me or allow me to be a leader.
_ I really want people to address me by my title or position.
_ I have a difficult time admitting when I make a mistake, especially regarding my leadership.
_ I will often do something others want me to even when I know that it might not be for the best.
_ I find myself spending much of my time as a leader simply reacting to the needs and crises of others.
_ I often neglect to take a day off because people urgently need me.
_ I find it very difficult when people criticize or reject me.
_ **Total**

Look at your totals in each of the four areas above and take some time to assess before God how significant an issue each area is for you.

We would suggest that a total of 40–50 in an area indicates that this area is definitely an issue for you; 30–40 indicates it is probably an issue for you; 20–30 indicates it may be an issue for you; and less than 20 suggests it is probably not an issue for you.

The "Nudge" Test

Pause and listen to the Holy Spirit. Do you feel a "nudge" that perhaps you have sought identity, significance, security, or acceptance in your leadership?

Pray the following prayer in light of what God has shown you above:

Dear Heavenly Father,

I confess that I have sinned against You in how I have sought my identity, significance, security, and acceptance in leadership roles, positions, and titles rather than in my relationship with You. In particular, I confess that I have sought my identity, significance, security, or acceptance outside of You in the following ways: ______________________________ (list what the Holy Spirit has shown you or brings to your mind now). I acknowledge that this is sin. Thank you that in Christ I am forgiven. I renounce seeking my identity, significance, security, and acceptance in these ways. I choose to base my life in You alone, through faith in Your Son Jesus Christ. Please fill me with Your Spirit and help me trust in You alone. Through Jesus Christ, my Lord. Amen.

Part 2 – Affirming Who We Are in Christ as Leaders

God loves us and wants us to be firmly rooted in Christ, and that must happen before we can freely lead others. Trying to discover who we are in leadership roles, and hoping such roles will make us more significant, secure, and accepted can only lead to disaster. On the other hand, leading others can be very fulfilling if we are deeply rooted in Christ. Read the following affirmations aloud and let the Word of God dwell richly within you:

My Identity In Christ Affirmed

I renounce the lie that I depend on any leadership role for my significance, because in Christ I am deeply significant. God says that:

I am the salt of the earth and the light of the world (see Matthew 5:13, 14)

I am a branch of the true vine, Jesus, a channel of His life (see John 15:1, 5)

I have been chosen and appointed by God to bear fruit (see John 15:16)

I am a personal, Spirit empowered witness for Christ (see Acts 1:8)

I am a temple of God (see 1 Corinthians 3:16)

I am a minister of reconciliation for God (see 2 Corinthians 5:17–21)

I am Christ's ambassador to the world (see 2 Corinthians 5:20)

I am God's fellow worker (see 2 Corinthians 6:1)

I am seated with Christ in the heavenly realm (see Ephesians 2:6)

I am God's workmanship, created for good works (see Ephesians 2:10)

I may approach God with freedom and confidence (see Ephesians 3:12)

I can do all things through Christ who strengthens me! (see Philippians 4:13)

I renounce the lie that I depend on any leadership role for my security, because in Christ I am totally secure. God says that:

I am free forever from condemnation (see Romans 8:1, 2)

I am assured that all things work together for good (see Romans 8:28)

I am free from any condemning charges against me (see Romans 8:31–34)

I cannot be separated from the love of God (see Romans 8:35–39)

I have been established, anointed, and sealed by God (see 2 Corinthians 1:21, 22)

I am confident that the good work God has begun in me will be perfected (see Philippians 1:6)

I am a citizen of heaven (see Philippians 3:20)

I am hidden with Christ in God (see Colossians 3:3)

I have not been given a spirit of cowardice, but of power, love, and a sound mind (see 2 Timothy 1:7)

I can find grace and mercy to help in time of need (see Hebrews 4:16)

I am born of God and the evil one cannot touch me. (see 1 John 5:18)

I renounce the lie that I depend on any leadership role for my acceptance, because in Christ I am completely accepted. God says that:

I am God's child (see John 1:12)

I am Christ's friend (see John 15:5)

I have been justified (see Romans 5:1)

I am united with the Lord and I am one spirit with Him (see 1 Corinthians 6:17)

I have been bought with a price: I belong to God (see 1 Corinthians 6:19, 20)

I am a member of Christ's body (see 1 Corinthians 12:27)

I am a saint, a holy one (see Ephesians 1:1)

I have been adopted as God's child (see Ephesians 1:5)

I have direct access to God through the Holy Spirit (see Ephesians 2:18)

I have been redeemed and forgiven of all my sins (see Colossians 1:14)

I am complete in Christ. (see Colossians 2:10)

My Identity In Christ Declared

Now get together with one other person. Sit or stand directly opposite each other. Each person should read the following aloud to the other person. One person in turn should read the entire list to the other person. (If you are working through the Leadership Steps on your own, try looking at yourself in a mirror as you read these statements.)

I declare to you, _____________ (name), that you do not depend on any leadership role for your significance, because in Christ you are deeply significant. God says that:

You are the salt of the earth and the light of the world (see Matthew 5:13, 14)

You are a branch of the true vine, Jesus, a channel of His life (see John 15:1, 5)

You have been chosen and appointed by God to bear fruit (see John 15:16)

You are a personal, Spirit empowered witness for Christ (see Acts 1:8)

You are a temple of God (see 1 Corinthians 3:16)

You are a minister of reconciliation for God (see 2 Corinthians 5:17–21)

You are Christ's ambassador to the world (see 2 Corinthians 5:20)

You are God's fellow worker (see 2 Corinthians 6:1)

You are seated with Christ in the heavenly realm (see Ephesians 2:6)

You are God's workmanship, created for good works (see Ephesians 2:10)

You may approach God with freedom and confidence (see Ephesians 3:12)

You can do all things through Christ who strengthens you! (see Philippians 4:13)

I declare to you, _____________ (name), that you do not depend on any leadership role for your security, because in Christ you are totally secure. God says that:

You are free forever from condemnation (see Romans 8:1,2)

You are assured that all things work together for good (see Romans 8:28)

You are free from any condemning charges against you (Romans 8:31–34)

You cannot be separated from the love of God (see Romans 8:35–39)

You have been established, anointed, and sealed by God (see 2 Corinthians 1:21, 22)

You are confident that the good work God has begun in you will be perfected (Philippians 1:6)

You are a citizen of heaven (see Philippians 3:20)

You are hidden with Christ in God (see Colossians 3:3)

You have not been given a spirit of cowardice, but of power, love, and a sound mind (see 2 Timothy 1:7)

You can find grace and mercy to help in time of need (see Hebrews 4:16)

You are born of God and the evil one cannot touch you. (see 1 John 5:18)

I declare to you, _____________ (name), that you do not depend on any leadership role for your acceptance, because in Christ you are completely accepted. God says that:

You are God's child (see John 1:12)

You are Christ's friend (see John 15:5)

You have been justified (see Romans 5:1)

You are united with the Lord and you are one spirit with Him (see 1 Corinthians 6:17)

You have been bought with a price: You belong to God (see 1 Corinthians 6:19, 20)

You are a member of Christ's body (see 1 Corinthians 12:27)

You are a saint, a holy one (see Ephesians 1:1)

You have been adopted as God's child (see Ephesians 1:5)

You have direct access to God through the Holy Spirit (see Ephesians 2:18)

You have been redeemed and forgiven of all your sins (see Colossians 1:14)

You are complete in Christ. (see Colossians 2:10)

If you did the above with a partner, finish this step by praying for each other.

Step Two: Forgiveness in Leadership

Conflicts in leadership are inevitable. We will experience criticism, sabotage, ingratitude, and any number of pains and offences. Leaders who do not forgive will become bitter and angry and may ultimately experience burnout or other negative spiritual, mental, and physical outcomes.

Leaders must forgive others in order to relate to others in healthy ways and to maintain a healthy connection with both people and people-systems. However, we must forgive mainly for the sake of our own relationship with God (see Matthew 18:23–35). This Step will enable you to do that.

We are to forgive others as Christ has forgiven us. He did that by taking all the sins of the world upon Himself. Essentially, forgiving others is agreeing to live with the consequences of their sins. That may seem unfair, but we will have to anyway. The only real choice is to live in the bondage of bitterness, or forgive from our hearts others who have hurt us. It is for our own sake that we make that choice.

We forgive someone who has hurt us because the pain will not go away until we forgive. We don't heal damaged emotions in order to forgive. We forgive and our restored fellowship with God is what brings the healing.

Forgiveness does not mean tolerating sin. We have every right to set up scriptural boundaries to stop further abuse. Leaders who forgive their followers must still carry out discipline when appropriate. The difference is that they don't do it in the bitterness that would make it less effective.

Forgiveness does not necessarily mean that the other has done something wrong, but is merely an acknowledgement that the other has caused us pain. Of course, we do need to forgive when someone sins against us, but we also need to forgive when someone does something that is not sinful but causes us pain — such as when they give us godly correction.

As we forgive, we release the pain of what was said or done to us to God through Jesus Christ. Whenever the memory of what was said or done returns and causes pain again, we need to forgive again. As we continue to forgive, God will come and begin to heal the pain we have experienced. Forgiveness is not the same as reconciliation, although both are biblical concepts. If you have been wounded or sinned against, you have a responsibility to forgive (see Matthew 18:23–35 or Matthew 6:12–15). If you know you have wounded or sinned against someone else, you have a responsibility to seek reconciliation (see Matthew 5:23–26) – although either party may initiate reconciliation. As you go through this Step, the Lord might bring to your mind people with whom you need to initiate reconciliation. Make a list of them.

Begin with this prayer:

Dear Heavenly Father,

As a leader, I know that I have sinned many times. I have wounded others, knowingly and unknowingly. I thank You for the riches of Your kindness, forbearance, and patience towards me, knowing that Your kindness has led me to repentance. I confess that I have not shown that same kindness and patience towards those leaders or followers who have hurt or offended me. Instead, I have held on to my anger, bitterness, and resentment towards them. Please bring to my mind all the people I need to forgive who have wounded me either as a leader or a follower, in order that I may now choose to forgive. In Jesus' name. Amen.

(See Romans 2:4.)

List everyone the Lord brings to your mind – other leaders, followers, or anyone else who has wounded you:

Remember, it matters not whether these people have actually sinned against you. If you *feel* they have, the need to forgive them still exists. That is why many need to forgive God. Even though we know that God has not sinned, we may feel that He has let us down.

In order to forgive others from our hearts, we have to allow God to reach our emotional core and we need to acknowledge all hurtful and hateful feelings, especially the ones we have tried to suppress. God wants to surface such feelings so we can let them go. That happens when we forgive others for the specific things they have done that God brings to mind, and acknowledge how those things made us feel.

Forgiving yourself is actually acknowledging that God has forgiven you, but it is extremely helpful for some to say, "Lord I forgive myself for (tell God the mistakes you made and other things you are beating yourself up for)."

Forgiving others is a crisis of the will. Don't say, "Lord, I want to forgive" or "Lord, help me forgive". God will always help us. We *choose* to forgive people for specific things we believe they have done.

Pray the following prayer for each person on your list, and stay with that person until every painful memory has been acknowledged:

Lord, I choose to forgive ______________(name) for ______________(what they did or failed to do) which made me feel ______________(describe the pain).

After you have prayed through your list, pray the following:

Lord, I choose not to hold on to my resentment. I renounce all bitterness. I give up my right to seek revenge or to punish those who have wounded me. I thank You for setting me free from my bondage to bitterness and I ask You to heal my damaged emotions. I choose to bless those who have hurt me. In particular, I choose to bless ________________(name the people). In Jesus' name. Amen.

Reconciliation

List the names of all the people with whom you may need to seek reconciliation.

If we have sinned against another person, we need to go to that person and specifically ask them to forgive us for what we have done, or not done, and make restitution if it is called for (Matthew 5:23, 24). It is always better to do that personally rather than by letter, phone, or email. Begin the process of reconciliation now by praying as follows:

Almighty God, I confess that I sinned against __________(name of person) by __________(state what you did or said). By Your Holy Spirit, please show me how to seek reconciliation with this person. In Jesus' name I pray. Amen.

If you have said or done something that may have wounded the person but which was not necessarily sinful (such as speaking an appropriate word of correction), then use this prayer:

Dear Heavenly Father, I ask You to heal the wounds that I may have caused to __________(name of person) when I __________(state what you did or said). Please reveal to my mind any way that __________(state what you did or said) was sinful, so that I might repent. By Your Holy Spirit, please show me how to seek reconciliation with this person. In Jesus' name. Amen.

Be sure to follow through in any way the Lord shows you. Be patient in the process and note that reconciliation can never be guaranteed as it depends on the response of the other person (Romans 12:18). However, if you have forgiven them and sought their forgiveness, you will have peace with God. For much deeper discussion about reconciliation read Neil Anderson's book *Restoring Broken Relationships* (Bethany House Publishing, formerly *The Path to Reconciliation*, Regal Books).

Step Three: Overcoming Anxiety And Reactivity In Leadership

Anxiety disables leadership by immersing us in the problems and tensions around us in such a way that it prevents us from seeing God's truth and gaining perspective from God on how to move forward in obedience. Anxiety blinds leaders so that they lose any sense of vision and direction from God. Anxiety distorts our perspectives and our communication.

When leaders are anxious, they are more prone to reactive relationships: relationships where people instantly oppose one another and cease giving one another grace and forgiveness. In these relationships, we react out of our flesh instead of our spirits. Leaders can choose to respond thoughtfully and gracefully towards others who are reactive, especially those who oppose or criticize them personally. In order to do so, they must first recognize these relationships and choose to break the reactivity by responding in grace and love.

Part 1 – Overcoming Anxiety

Anxiety often operates in the background of our minds. The particular source(s) of anxiety may be any number of issues: too much to do; too much information to process; financial struggles; relationship struggles; problems at work; problems at home; etc. Often, several sources of anxiety may be operating at the same time. In order to overcome anxiety, we must ask the Holy Spirit to reveal the source(s) of anxiety. Then we need to repent of this anxiety, choosing to present the matter to God in prayer and thanksgiving. If the anxiety is deep-seated or chronic, we may need to do a "stronghold-busting" exercise to eliminate it (see the Freedom In Christ Discipleship Course for more information). To begin discerning anxiety in your life, pray the following:

Dear Heavenly Father,

You are the omniscient God. You know the thoughts and intentions of my heart. You know the situations I am in from the beginning to the end. I place my trust in You to supply all my needs according to Your riches in glory and to guide me into all truth. Please reveal to my mind all the emotions and symptoms that I have been experiencing which are evidence of anxiety in my life. In Jesus' name. Amen.

Tick the emotions and symptoms of anxiety below that are true for you. Add others that the Spirit brings to mind.

- ❑ General uneasiness or nervousness
- ❑ Impulsiveness
- ❑ Unforgiveness
- ❑ Defensiveness
- ❑ Lack of concentration
- ❑ Restlessness
- ❑ Hyperactivity
- ❑ Loss of creativity
- ❑ Not thinking clearly
- ❑ Highly emotional
- ❑ Loss of objectivity
- ❑ Procrastination
- ❑ Stubbornness
- ❑ Sense of helplessness or self-doubt
- ❑ Difficulty in making choices
- ❑ Vivid nightmares
- ❑ Blaming
- ❑ Criticism and judgmentalism
- ❑ Wilfulness
- ❑ Demanding your own way
- ❑ Gossip or rumours
- ❑ Feeling victimized
- ❑ Exaggeration
- ❑ Moodiness
- ❑ Miscommunication
- ❑ Too much TV or media
- ❑ Too much drink or food
- ❑ Money concerns
- ❑ Working too hard
- ❑ Others:

Selecting more than three indicates that anxiety may be a problem. More than seven suggests that you may be chronically anxious.

Pray the following prayer:

Loving Father,

Your Word tells us not to be anxious, but I realize that I have not obeyed Your Word. I have allowed myself to be anxious about many things, as the emotions and symptoms above have shown me. I confess that my anxiety shows a lack of trust in You. I now ask You to search me, O God, and know my heart; try me and know my anxious thoughts; and see if there be any hurtful way in me, and lead me in the everlasting way. Please reveal to my mind all sources of anxiety that I might commit each of them to You in trust and obedience. In Jesus' precious name. Amen.

(Matthew 6:31–34; Philippians 4:6; Psalm 139:23, 24)

1. List the sources of anxiety (evidenced by the emotions and symptoms above) that the Holy Spirit reveals to your mind, being as specific as possible:

(Example: I have so much to do that I'm afraid I will miss something important.)

2. For each source of anxiety, describe what You are believing or assuming (these are generally "lies") that is causing you apprehension or emotional pain.

(Example: I need to do everything I'm doing.)

Respond with this prayer:

Dear Heavenly Father,

I choose to trust in You alone. I do not trust in myself or my own abilities to resolve the situations in my life. I do not trust in my relatives and friends to resolve the situations in my life. I do not trust in my work to resolve the situations in my life. I do not trust my church to resolve the situations in my life. I choose to trust in You alone. I now commit the following sources of anxiety to You in prayer:

1. List the anxiety or source of anxiety.
2. Describe the emotions or symptoms that accompany it.
3. Pray for the appropriate resolution or outcome.

In the name of Jesus Christ, I now renounce the lies that I have believed about these sources of anxiety. In particular, I renounce the lie that: __________(list each lie you have believed or assumed).

Thank You that You are sovereign over my life. Thank You that You are in control of the situations of my life. Thank You that You always work for my good in every situation. Thank You that through Jesus Christ I am not a victim of anxiety, but I am an overcomer of anxiety. I choose to walk in obedience to You, resisting anxiety by keeping my focus on You. Through Jesus Christ. Amen.

Part 2 – Breaking Cycles Of Reactivity

Reactivity cycles occur whenever we become stuck in a relationship where we are opposing, resisting, and criticizing the other. We become reactive when we begin to engage with other people out of our flesh, that sinful aspect of our humanity that resists God's will. When we are reactive, others often become reactive to us as well, entrapping us in a reactivity cycle.

We may become reactive not only towards individuals, but also towards groups and organizations. For example, people can become reactive towards a political party, so that no matter what the leader of a certain political party might say these people will find something to oppose. This may lead to intractable disagreements among people regarding politics, which prevent people from working together for the good of their country.

At any time, we can break reactivity cycles by persistently choosing to respond to the other out of grace, love, and forgiveness. Respond to God as you pray this prayer:

Dear Heavenly Father,

Your Word says that You are merciful and gracious, slow to anger, and abounding in steadfast love (Exodus 34:6). Although I have received Your mercy, I confess that I have not always extended this mercy to others. Instead, I have allowed myself to react out of my flesh. Please reveal to my mind anyone with whom I have been reactive, so that I might repent and find freedom. In Jesus' name. Amen.

1. List each person that the Spirit brings to Your mind.

2. For each person, describe how you have been reactive towards that person.

3. For each person, pray the following prayer:

Lord,

I confess that I have been reactive towards __________(name the person or group) by __________(describe the ways in which you have been reactive). Thank You that in Christ I am forgiven. I now choose to respond to __________(name the person or group) in grace, love, and mercy. I choose to give __________(name the person or group) grace as You have given grace to me through Your Son Jesus Christ. I ask that You would make me an agent of reconciliation with (name the person or group). I choose to bless (name the person or group) in the name of Jesus Christ, my Lord. Amen.

(Ephesians 4:32)

As appropriate, you may need to seek reconciliation with those on your list (see Step 2). Allow the Holy Spirit to lead you in this. Often, as we choose to break the cycle of reactivity, reconciliation with that person naturally begins to occur by the Holy Spirit.

Step Four: Embracing Our Leadership Responsibility

The purpose of this Step is to help us understand and embrace who God has created us to be as leaders, whether we are a natural leader, a leader in our people-system, or a leader in a particular situation. Natural leaders are people who lead as a matter of course, no matter what context they seem to be in. Their normal disposition is leadership. Other leaders may be called to lead in a particular people-system (group of people). They may be leaders at home or at work, but they do not generally lead outside their people-system. Almost everyone will need to lead from time to time as the situation requires. Because almost everyone will lead from time to time, there is not an activity for discernment in this aspect of leadership.

After helping identify how you are called to leadership, this Step then helps you resolve the times when you have failed to exercise leadership or when you have exercised leadership in the wrong way. If we fail to lead as God requires or if we exercise our leadership in the wrong way, then we have sinned. So we must resolve these areas of sin if we are to lead appropriately.

Part 1 – Identifying The Scope Of Your Leadership

Dear Heavenly Father,

I rejoice that You have saved me by grace through faith, and that I am Your workmanship created in Christ Jesus for good works that You have prepared for me (Ephesians 2:8–10). I know that You have created each person differently, and You have given each person different spiritual gifts, callings, and ministries by Your Holy Spirit (1 Corinthians 12:4–7). I pray that You would reveal to my mind how you have created me and called me to lead. In Jesus' name. Amen.

Natural Leadership

Please rate the following statements on a scale of 1 to 10, with 10 being the highest:

_ No matter whether I am at work, church, home, or other organizations, I find that people consistently ask me to lead.
_ Whenever I am leading, I feel confident.
_ Whenever I am leading, I feel positive.
_ Whenever I am leading, I feel energized.
_ I usually serve more effectively by leading a team than I do as a general team member.
_ I generally do not feel threatened or jealous when I am around other leaders.
_ People seem to enjoy following my leadership.
_ The best way I can serve people is by leading them.
_ I find it relatively easy to get a clear vision from God for my work, church, home, or other organization of which I am part.
_ I can point to a record of good fruit stemming from contexts in which I was leading.
_ **Total**

If your score is 70 or above, it is likely that God has called you as a natural leader. (It is often best to verify your responses with your spouse or a close friend, who can assist you in your discernment.)

Once you have completed this exercise, pray the following:

Dear Heavenly Father,

Thank you for creating me to be the leader that I am, whether or not I am a natural leader. I surrender to Your purpose in my life regarding leadership. I affirm that Your Son Jesus was the greatest leader of all, the perfect example of genuine leadership. By Your Spirit, I choose to follow His example of leadership, using leadership to serve others in humility. May my leadership always reflect and be filled with the life of Jesus. Amen.

People-System Leadership

Review the list of people-systems below. Put a tick next to those in which you already serve as a leader or you believe God is calling you to serve as a leader. Write a note next to any people-system that requires additional specification (e.g. "budget team at work" or "Girl Guides troop").

- ❑ Your immediate family
- ❑ Your extended family
- ❑ Your work
- ❑ Teams or other groups at work
- ❑ Your profession or professional associations
- ❑ Your church
- ❑ Church cell group/home group
- ❑ Community and social organizations
- ❑ Others:

Pray the following in light of your answers above:

Dear Heavenly Father,

I thank You for the person You have created me to be. I now freely and wholeheartedly choose to walk in the ways You have prepared for me, accepting the leadership responsibilities You have given me. In particular, I affirm that You have called me to lead in __________(list all specific contexts). By Your Holy Spirit, empower me to serve others through my leadership in whatever people-systems or situations You place me, so that I might bring glory and honour to my Lord Jesus Christ. Amen.

Part 2 – Identifying Situations And People-Systems In Which You Failed To Lead

Every leader makes mistakes; every leader fails. This part of the Step focuses on times when we have neglected our leadership responsibilities or times in which we sought to fulfil our leadership responsibilities in a sinful way. Begin by praying the following prayer:

Dear Heavenly Father,

I thank you for Your mercy and kindness, knowing that Your kindness leads me to repentance (Romans 2:4). I confess that I have not always led when I have needed to lead, neglecting my responsibility before You. I also confess that I have not always led in the way I should lead, but have led out of selfish motives and in sinful ways. Please reveal to my mind any and all ways that I have not led as You have wanted, so that I might repent. In Jesus' name. Amen.

1. List the people-systems above in which you have failed to lead as God wanted:

2. List the situations in which you have neglected your leadership responsibilities or have failed to lead as needed:

3. List the situations in which you have led wrongly:

4. Put a mark next to any of the following that are true for you:

- ❑ I have used guilt or shame to get others to do what I want or think best.
- ❑ I have demanded that others do what I want or follow my rules.
- ❑ I have controlled others by my strong personality, heavy-handed persuasion, or the use of fear or intimidation.
- ❑ I have expected to be in charge because I am the leader.
- ❑ I have tried to get others to do what I want using rules, regulations, and standards.
- ❑ I have striven to get or maintain a position or role in order to accomplish my agenda.
- ❑ I have assumed responsibility for the lives and well-being of other adults under my leadership.
- ❑ I have driven others and myself harder and harder in order to achieve the vision.
- ❑ I have been stubborn and rigid in my leadership.
- ❑ I have required people under my leadership to do what I say, when I say it and how I say it.
- ❑ I have expected others to work as hard as I do if they want my approval.
- ❑ I have never been really satisfied with the performance of others I lead.
- ❑ Other things the Lord may show you:

Pray the following prayer, including the items you have listed above:

Lord, I confess that I have not led when I should have. Specifically, I confess my sins in these areas: __________(list the ones indicated in 1 and 2 above). I also confess that I have led wrongly. Specifically, I confess these wrong ways of leading: __________(list the ones indicated in 3 or 4 above). Thank You that in Jesus Christ I am forgiven. I now commit myself to leading in whatever situation You ask and in a manner worthy of Jesus Christ, the greatest leader of all. Amen.

Conclude this Step with the following prayer:

Gracious and loving God,

Thank You for allowing me to serve people through leadership as the person I am in Christ. I pray that I might fulfil all my leadership responsibilities humbly, joyfully, and lovingly, in the manner of Your Son, Jesus. Empower me by Your Holy Spirit to live in obedience to You and serve in love. Through Jesus Christ. Amen.

Step Five: Money, Sex, And Power In Leadership

When a leader fails, most often it is because of one (or more) of the following: money, sex, and power. When any of these three things are out of balance in our lives, it will undermine our leadership ability. This will be true even if the issue does not seem to be directly related to our leadership context. This Step asks the Holy Spirit to reveal to our minds all ways that we have sinned or are sinning in each of these areas.

Part 1 – Money

When we use the term "money", we are referring to all the financial and material resources (car, home, computer, etc.) God has provided for us. In this Step, we are asking God to reveal not only our behaviours but also our attitudes concerning our financial and material resources. Greed is the desire to have more and more or to have more than you actually need. Covetousness is the longing to possess things that other people have. Envy is a feeling of discontent or resentful longing arising from someone else's situation.

Begin with this prayer:

Dear Heavenly Father,

I thank You that You richly supply me with all the resources I need through Your Son Jesus Christ. You have said that the love of money is the root of all kinds of evil (1 Timothy 6:10). Because of this, You have told us to keep our lives free from the love of money and choose to be content with what we have (Hebrews 13:5). You have promised that if we seek first Your kingdom, then You would add to us all the things we need (Matthew 6:33). I confess that I have not always done this. Instead, I have sinned through greed, envy, and covetousness. I have also sinned by failing to be a good steward of the financial and material resources that You have supplied to me. I now ask You to reveal to my mind any and all ways that I have sinned regarding money, that I might fully repent. In Jesus' name. Amen.

Ways that we may sin as leaders regarding money:

- ❑ Failing to live within my means or according to a budget
- ❑ Not paying off my credit cards each month or carrying a large balance on my credit cards with no ability to pay them off
- ❑ Having large amounts of consumer debt
- ❑ Taking small items from my workplace for my personal use
- ❑ Failing to file or pay my taxes on time and in full
- ❑ Trying to disguise money problems that I may be having
- ❑ Failing to exercise good stewardship of the resources God has given me (e.g. failing to maintain my car or my home, failing to care for my computer and phone, etc.)
- ❑ Using or administering the financial resources of my workplace without transparency and appropriate financial controls
- ❑ Failing to insist that others use appropriate financial controls and stewardship of our common resources (at home, in the workplace, or in church)
- ❑ Ignoring financial practices that I know to be wrong (for myself, at home, in the workplace, or in church)
- ❑ Feeling rebellious or defensive when I'm asked to give appropriate account for my financial activities and expenditures
- ❑ Failing to ensure that my current account and savings account balance each month
- ❑ Finding myself practising "retail therapy" or conspicuous consumption
- ❑ Envying or coveting the resources of other friends, co-workers or leaders in similar situations to myself
- ❑ Finding it difficult to share my financial needs with others who may be able to help me
- ❑ Failing to give financially as God has instructed me
- ❑ Spending a lot of time thinking and worrying about money matters
- ❑ Being overly concerned about getting the financial remuneration that I feel I deserve
- ❑ Feeling that I am entitled to a certain level of financial remuneration
- ❑ Other ways that God is showing me:

Respond to what God has shown you by praying this prayer:

Dear Heavenly Father,

I thank You for the riches of Your kindness towards me, leading me to turn away from my sin. I confess that I have sinned regarding money in the following ways: ________(list them). Thank You that in Jesus Christ I am forgiven. I choose to turn away from my sin and exercise good stewardship over the financial and material resources that You have entrusted to me as a person and as a leader. Help me to be faithful in little, so that I may receive much to use for Your kingdom (Luke 16:10–12). Through Jesus, my Lord. Amen.

Part 2 – Sex

In this section, we are not looking to deal with all the ways that we have sinned regarding sex, but we are focusing primarily on our leadership context. However, it is important that we repent of all immoral sexual activity according to the Bible and ensure that we resolve all outstanding personal and spiritual issues regarding our sexuality. (See *The Steps To Freedom In Christ*, Step 6, for guidance on how to resolve issues regarding immoral sexual activity more fully.) In this Step, we are asking God to reveal not only our behaviours but also our attitudes regarding sexual issues.

Pray the following:

Dear Heavenly Father,

I thank You that sex is Your good gift to be exercised according to Your Word in the covenant of marriage between one man and one woman. I acknowledge that immoral sexual activity includes a range of sins that undermine our relationship with You and with others. I confess that it ruins our ability to lead as Christians. I now ask You to bring to my mind any sexual sin in thought, word, or action that I might repent of these sexual sins and break their bondages. In Jesus' name. Amen.

Ways that we may sin as leaders regarding sex:

- ❑ Thinking about co-workers or those I lead in a lustful way
- ❑ Looking at co-workers or those I lead in a lustful way
- ❑ Looking at pornography
- ❑ "Channel surfing" or internet surfing when I am tired or stressed
- ❑ Watching films and TV programmes that contain strong sexual images
- ❑ Daydreaming about immoral sexual activity
- ❑ Finding myself longing to spend time with people of the opposite gender (who I am not either dating or married to), especially in one-to-one circumstances
- ❑ Not taking time to develop healthy friendships with people of the same gender
- ❑ Thinking too much about past relationships, especially if they involved immoral sexual contact
- ❑ Dwelling on temptations towards homosexuality or paedophilia
- ❑ Not giving sufficient attention and effort to nurturing my sexual relationship with my spouse
- ❑ Using sex with my spouse as a means of fulfilling my sinful lust
- ❑ Other ways that God is showing me:

Once you have considered this list, choose to repent by praying this prayer:

Dear Heavenly Father,

I admit that I have not always exercised self-control and obedience to You and Your Word regarding my sexuality. I confess that I have sinned against You by __________ (list them). I renounce all these sexual sins, and I admit to any wilful participation. I choose now to present my eyes, mouth, mind, heart, hands, feet, and sexual organs to You as instruments of righteousness. I present my whole body to You as a living sacrifice, holy and acceptable. I choose to reserve the sexual use of my body for marriage only (see Hebrews 13:4). I now loose myself from any sinful bonds I have made with any co-worker or follower in my heart or in my behaviour. In the name of the Lord Jesus Christ, I cancel any effects my sin has on my leadership and take back any ground I have given to the

devil. Thank You that You have totally cleansed and forgiven me and that You love and accept me just the way I am. Therefore, I choose now to present myself and my body to You as clean in Your eyes. In Jesus' name. Amen.

Part 3 – Power

Power is a complex concept in leadership. Leaders have authority and responsibility for people in order that people may experience God's best for them. However, as leaders we can often use our authority and responsibility as a means to control and manipulate others. Most leaders unintentionally fall into this from time to time. A few leaders consciously choose to control others. Some leaders will try to control others because they enjoy having positions of power and influence. Other leaders try to control people out of fear and self-protection. Some people will seek positions of leadership in order to use these positions of leadership to achieve their own desires or their own agenda.

In this section, we are asking God to reveal to us all the ways that we have sought to control or manipulate people using our leadership. Begin with this prayer:

Almighty God, You are the Sovereign Lord of all creation. We know that nothing is outside the control of Your Son Jesus Christ, even though it does not always seem that everything is under His control. Lord Jesus, You uphold the universe by Your power. As Your people, the power we have comes by Your Holy Spirit and through godliness. Your power is at work within us, but it enables us to live fully for You. You have not given us power over others. It is the love of Christ that controls us, and You do not allow us to control others. Instead, You call us to self-control. I confess that I have used my leadership as a means to gain or exercise power over others. I repent of this sin and ask You to reveal to my mind all the ways that I have used my leadership as a means to control others. Please reveal all the ways that I have become intoxicated with my power and position over others. In Jesus' name. Amen.

(See Hebrews 2:8; Hebrews 1:3; 2 Timothy 3:5; 2 Timothy 1:7; Ephesians 3:20; 2 Corinthians 5:14.)

Ways that we may sin as leaders regarding power and control:

- ❑ Expecting (or trying to force) people to follow me because of my position, title, degrees, or achievements
- ❑ Using guilt or shame to persuade others to do what I think is right
- ❑ Using biblical verses such as "Touch not my anointed ones" (Psalm 105:15) to defend myself or persuade others
- ❑ Not sharing requested or needed information in an open and timely manner
- ❑ Withholding pertinent information needed by my co-workers or followers
- ❑ Acting or speaking in deceptive ways in order to control others or protect myself
- ❑ Spending time and energy trying to control people and situations instead of exercising self-control
- ❑ Using harsh or judgmental language with others, especially when I want them to do something
- ❑ Threatening others with bad consequences in order to get my way
- ❑ Threatening others with my own resignation or withdrawal in order to get my way
- ❑ Having the tendency to think that my way is the right way
- ❑ Giving people responsibility but expecting them to fulfil it in the way I determine
- ❑ Not allowing, actively or passively, other people to take leadership responsibility as appropriate
- ❑ Not giving people open access to the resources needed in order to fulfil their responsibilities fully and in a timely way
- ❑ Giving different people different information about the same activity, responsibility or situation
- ❑ Using rules, regulations, or the Bible in a way that stifles discussion and tries to force people to listen to me or obey me
- ❑ Using phrases such as "because I said so" or "the Lord told me" when people raise questions about my decisions or opinions
- ❑ Using technical, obscure or complicated language in order to persuade people that I am right
- ❑ Being harsh, critical, or abusive with others, especially if they do not agree with me
- ❑ Taking responsibility for someone else's obedience and discipleship
- ❑ Other ways that God may be showing you:

Pray the following:

Almighty God,

I confess that I have used my leadership as a means to control people and situations. In particular, I confess __________ (list them). I renounce all ways and means of using leadership to control others, especially the ones that I have listed. Thank You that in Jesus I am forgiven. I cancel all ground gained in my life through my sin in this area. I choose to lead in the way of Jesus, who for our sakes emptied Himself and made Himself nothing, becoming the servant of all (Philippians 2:5ff.). Fill me with Your Holy Spirit, that I might live for You. In Jesus' name. Amen.

Step Six: Renouncing Pride, Defensiveness, And Selfish Ambition In Leadership

This Step addresses three key areas that deeply affect leadership: pride, defensiveness, and selfish ambition. These three factors are at the root of the lack of healthy unity, not only in the Church but also in the workplace. These factors cause a lot of dysfunction and disease among leaders as well as followers. They prevent people and people-systems from working together effectively for the benefit of society.

Part 1 – Pride

Pride is one of the great leadership sins. Pride involves having a high opinion of oneself or one's importance, which can show itself in many ways. Pride often puts leaders in situations where people will oppose, resist, or resent them. Pride always puts leaders in opposition to God. Left unchecked, pride functions like a cancer in leadership, eating away at our leadership until it dies. Even many secular books and authorities on leadership recognize the destructive influence of pride in a leader.

Begin with the following prayer:

Dear Heavenly Father, You have said that pride goes before destruction and an arrogant spirit before a fall. As a leader, I confess that I have often considered myself more highly than I ought. I have wanted to be first and not last. I have chosen to serve myself, seeking my own desires and disguising it as serving others. As a result, I have given ground to the devil in my life and I have compromised my leadership. I have sinned by believing I could know and choose what is best for others on my own. In so doing, I have placed my will before Yours, and I have centred my life around myself instead of You.

I repent of my pride and selfishness in leadership and pray that all ground gained in me by the enemies of the Lord Jesus Christ would be cancelled. I choose to rely on the Holy Spirit's power and guidance so I will do nothing from selfishness or empty conceit. With humility of mind, I will seek to lead by Your Holy Spirit with the love and grace of Jesus.

Please show me now all the specific ways in which I have led in pride. Enable me through love to serve others and in honour to prefer others. I ask all of this in the gentle and humble name of Jesus, my Lord. Amen.

(See Proverbs 16:18; Matthew 6:33; 16:24; Romans 12:10; Philippians 2:3.)

Allow the Holy Spirit to show you any specific ways in which pride has infected your leadership. As the Lord brings to your mind areas of pride, use the prayer below to guide you in your confession.

Ways that pride might become evident in leadership:

- ❑ Having or showing a stubborn and determined intention to do what I think is best
- ❑ Leading from my own understanding and experience rather than patiently seeking God's guidance through prayer and His Word
- ❑ Leading from my own energy and effort instead of depending on the power of the Holy Spirit
- ❑ Leading in ways that control or manipulate others instead of using self-control
- ❑ Having impatience when it comes to seeing the change or getting the outcomes I want in my leadership contexts
- ❑ Being too busy doing important things as a leader to take time to do little things for others
- ❑ Having a tendency to think that I do not need anyone's help to lead
- ❑ Finding it hard to admit when I am wrong
- ❑ Being more concerned about pleasing people than pleasing God with my leadership
- ❑ Being concerned about getting the credit I feel I deserve as a leader
- ❑ Thinking that as a leader I am more humble, spiritual, religious, or devoted than others
- ❑ Being driven to obtain recognition for my leadership abilities, especially because of the size or scope of my leadership responsibilities
- ❑ Feeling that my needs are not as important as others' needs so that I must sacrifice myself
- ❑ Feeling that others do not have the same level of commitment or ability in leadership as me
- ❑ Often feeling that if I do not do something as a leader then no one else will
- ❑ Thinking that I must keep things going as a leader otherwise they may fall apart

- ❑ Considering myself better than others because of my accomplishments or position as a leader
- ❑ Other ways I have thought more highly of myself than I should:

For each of the above areas that has been true in your life, pray:

Lord, I agree I have been proud by __________(list the ways). Thank You for forgiving me for my pride. I choose to renounce pride and humble myself before You and others. I choose to place all my confidence in You and none in my flesh. In Jesus' name. Amen.

Part 2 – Defending Ourselves Wrongly

Self-defence can be another sign of pride in a leader, or it may reflect that the leader is seeking his or her significance, security or acceptance in leadership. Self-defence is always problematic: if we have done something wrong, we have no defence; if we have not done anything wrong, we need no defence because God will defend us. Defensiveness will always undermine leadership, especially by undermining other people's trust in the leader. Pray the following:

Dear Heavenly Father,

You have promised to be my shelter and my fortress. By Your grace, You surround me and defend me. I admit that I have not always trusted in You as my defender. Instead, because of pride or insecurity, I have often struggled as a leader to admit that I was wrong or that I made a mistake. I have resisted attempts by others to show me my faults in accordance with Your Word. I have chosen to defend myself wrongly. In so doing I have wounded others and myself and I have offended You. Please reveal to my mind any ways that I have failed to trust You by trying to defend myself wrongly. In the name of Jesus. Amen.

Ways we defend ourselves wrongly:

- ❑ Pretending or thinking that I have not done anything wrong
- ❑ Pretending or thinking that my behaviour is better than it really is
- ❑ Focusing on my own best motives and another's worst behaviours
- ❑ Denying or distorting reality, evidence, or the truth
- ❑ Retreating into entertainment, drugs, alcohol, or food
- ❑ Trying to portray myself in a better light than others
- ❑ Withdrawing from people or keeping people at a distance
- ❑ Regressing to less threatening times or to immature attitudes and behaviours
- ❑ Showing displaced anger or irritability
- ❑ Projecting my problems on to others; blaming others for my problems; shifting the focus on to others
- ❑ Rationalizing my behaviour or my circumstances
- ❑ Lying, disguising the truth, or giving partial truths
- ❑ Presenting a false image of myself or my motives
- ❑ Framing motives, behaviours, attitudes, and situations in ways that are deceptive or that present myself as better than I am
- ❑ Adopting a martyr complex
- ❑ Adopting a messiah complex
- ❑ Adopting a hermit complex
- ❑ Showing a lack of openness and transparency
- ❑ Refusing to trust and release others
- ❑ Other ways that the Holy Spirit may show you:

In light of the above, pray the following:

Gracious Lord,

I confess that I have defended myself wrongly by __________ (list them). Thank You for Your forgiveness. I choose to trust You to defend and protect me. In Jesus' name. Amen.

Part 3 – Selfish Ambition, Envy, And Jealousy

Envy, jealousy and selfish ambition are three related sins. They lead to unholy comparisons with others and unrighteous competition. These sins are related to the sin of pride (see Philippians 2:3). In a sense, jealousy is an intensification of envy, and selfish ambition is an intensification of jealousy. This part of the Step seeks to reveal these sins in our lives so that we might repent.

There are four primary sources of envy, jealousy, and selfish ambition. First, people may feel or fear that they are being displaced in terms of their relationships with others or in terms of their status (position or influence) in their leadership context. Second, feeling insecure (or having our sense of security in someone other than Jesus) may lead to these sins. Third, people may develop an entitlement mentality, believing that they deserve something (especially something someone else has) because of their own efforts. Finally, these sins may result from an unwillingness to pay the price for – or trying to find a shortcut to get – what one wants. All these flow from pride and conceit. They may all be corrected by finding our significance, security, and acceptance in Jesus rather than our leadership.

Envy

Envy is a feeling of discontent or resentful longing aroused by someone else's possessions, qualities, or circumstances – including God's blessings. Envy is related to covetousness. Envy refers to wanting what someone else has. Ultimately, it will seek to destroy the one who is envied. Envy leads to rivalry, divisions, and quarrels (see Mark 15:10; Galatians 5:18–21; Philippians 1:15). Pray the following:

Dear Heavenly Father,

You have promised to supply all our needs according to Your riches in glory in Christ Jesus. You have commanded us not to desire what others have, whether it is relationships or property, talents or resources. Such envy is a work of the flesh, not the Spirit. I confess that as a leader I have often envied what other leaders have. I ask You to reveal to my mind all the ways that I have envied others, so that I might repent. In Jesus' name. Amen. (See Philippians 4:19; Exodus 20:17; Galatians 5:21.)

Some ways that we envy as leaders:

- ❑ Longing for the financial resources of another
- ❑ Longing for the material resources of another
- ❑ Feeling that if I only had what someone else had, then I would be successful or happy
- ❑ Longing for the relationships of another
- ❑ Longing to be like another in terms of talents, abilities, spiritual gifts, skills
- ❑ Longing for the leadership position of another
- ❑ Feeling resentful towards others because of what they have
- ❑ Not feeling content with what God has provided me
- ❑ Feeling that I need to work harder or smarter in order to get what others have
- ❑ Other ways the Holy Spirit may show you:

Once you have considered the items above, pray the following:

Gracious God,

I confess that I have sinned by envying others. Specifically, I have envied others by: __________(list them, being as specific as possible). I repent of my envy. Thank You that in Jesus I am forgiven. I ask You to wash me clean from the stain of envy. I choose to trust You and rejoice in Your provision for me. I choose to be content with what I have, knowing that You will use what I have to bring glory to Your Son Jesus. In His name I pray. Amen.

Jealousy

Jealousy is feeling or showing resentment towards someone because of that person's achievements, successes, perceived advantages, or relationships. Whereas envy focuses on what another has, jealousy focuses on the other person. Like envy, jealousy usually leads to quarrels and strife. Left unchecked, jealousy becomes an unholy zeal directed against another.

(There is a holy jealousy based on covenant faithfulness. This jealousy is aroused when someone gives to another the loyalty and affection belonging to one in covenant relationship. For example, when God's people worship idols or when a wife has affections for a man not her husband. See Exodus 20:5.)

Begin with this prayer:

Holy God,

Your Word says that You are a jealous God, calling us to a faithful love for You. At the same time, Your Word says that jealousy in us is a work of the flesh leading to arguments and dissensions. I confess that I have often resented other leaders because of their positions and accomplishments. I have sometimes even harboured ill will against them. This is sin. I ask You to reveal to my mind all the ways that I have been jealous and all the people of whom I have been jealous, so that I might repent. Through Jesus Christ, my Lord. Amen.

Ways that we can be jealous as leaders:

- ❑ Feeling that if I only had the same advantages as other leaders then I would have their accomplishments
- ❑ Feeling resentment towards others because of the relationships they have or enjoy
- ❑ Having hard feelings towards others because they have unfair advantages over me
- ❑ Feeling discontented because of the successes of others
- ❑ Secretly hoping that another leader would fail
- ❑ Feeling disgruntled with God because of the relationships others seem to enjoy with Him
- ❑ Other ways the Holy Spirit may show you:

People of whom I have been jealous:

Write the names of people and organizations the Lord shows you.

Reflecting on your answers above, pray this prayer:

Almighty God,

I confess that I have committed the sin of jealousy. I confess that I have been jealous by _________(list them). Thank You that in Jesus Christ I am forgiven. Cleanse me completely from the sin of jealousy.

I now ask You to bless abundantly all those I have been jealous of: _________(list the people). I ask You to heal any relationships broken because of jealousy, especially my relationship with _________(list them).

Thank You for saving me by Your grace. Thank You for who I am in Your Son, Jesus Christ. Thank You that I am Your child and that You love me fully and completely. I rejoice in Your love for me. I choose now to walk in the good works that You have prepared for me to do. Help me love You faithfully. Through Jesus. Amen.

Selfish Ambition

Zeal or ambition can be a good trait in a leader. Leaders with a healthy sense of ambition will seek to achieve great things for God, for people and for their organizations. Such zeal is a healthy, godly quality that inspires leaders for excellence. Leaders with a healthy sense of ambition will not care who gets the credit as long as the godly outcomes are achieved. Leaders with a healthy zeal will put others first and promote their well-being.

Selfish ambition is not the same as healthy ambition. Selfish ambition is a desire to put oneself forward as deserving of something someone else has. It flows from envy and jealousy. It is self-seeking instead of serving others. Selfish ambition is a partisan and factious spirit that will do almost anything to get its way and to get ahead. As such, selfish ambition always leads to a sense of rivalry and unholy competition with others. Selfish ambition is always destructive, leading to many evil practices (see James 3:14–16). When leaders become selfishly ambitious, they ultimately destroy themselves, other people, and sometimes the very organizations they lead.

Pray this prayer for discernment of selfish ambition in your life:

Loving Father,

You have told us to do nothing out of selfish ambition or vain conceit, but in humility of mind to count others as more significant (Philippians 2:3). I know that in Christ I am significant. However, I have repeatedly tried to find my sense of significance in other things. I confess that I have often sought my sense of significance in comparison and in competition with other leaders. I have allowed envy or jealousy to lead to a spirit of rivalry. This is sin. Please reveal to me all the ways that I have been selfishly ambitious, that I may repent. Also reveal to my mind all those with whom I have had an unhealthy rivalry and sense of competition. Through Jesus, my Lord. Amen.

Ways selfish ambition can manifest in our lives:

- ❑ Having a strong sense of competition regarding something that is not normally competitive (such as a game or a sport)
- ❑ Striving against another person
- ❑ Acting in ways that seem to set people against each other or seem to create disunity
- ❑ Comparing oneself with others in terms of numbers and quantities (e.g. size of budget, number of church members, scope of responsibilities)
- ❑ Thinking myself significant because I have a larger _________ (ministry, budget, workload, membership, etc.) than another leader
- ❑ Speaking or acting in ways that criticize, undermine, disparage, tear down, or in other ways harm another leader or his/her organization, ministry, achievements, etc.
- ❑ Speaking or acting in ways that harm another leader's relationships
- ❑ Other ways the Holy Spirit may show you:

List all the leaders and organizations with which you have developed an unhealthy rivalry or sense of competition:

Using your answers above, pray this prayer:

Gracious God,

Although I have been created and called by You for leadership, I have not led as You desire. I realize that I have not led by the wisdom that is pure, peaceable, gentle, open to reason, full of mercy and good fruits, impartial, and sincere (James 3:14–17). Instead, I have harboured selfish ambition in my heart by: __________(list them). In all these ways I have sought to put myself forward and advance my own agenda. I have not served others, but I have harmed others with my competition and rivalry. Thank You that in Christ I am forgiven. I ask You to cleanse me completely from every trace of selfish ambition. I ask You to bless and give success to all the other leaders around me, in particular __________(list them). I pray that You would heal any damage I have done through my selfish ambition. By the grace of Jesus. Amen.

The Holy Spirit may ask you to go to leaders in connection with whom you have had selfish ambition in order to seek reconciliation and in order to bless that leader.

Close this Step with this declaration:

I here and now, in the name and authority of the Lord Jesus Christ, renounce all envy, jealousy, and selfish ambition. I choose to rejoice in God's provision for me, in the person God has made me to be as His child, and in where God has called and placed me as a leader (Luke 10:20). In Jesus' name, I cancel all ground gained by Satan in my life, my leadership, my ministry, my work, and the organizations of which I am part because of my envy, jealousy, and selfish ambition. In Jesus' name, I now break every unholy bond I have created with people __________(list any that come to mind) through envy, jealousy, and selfish ambition.

In humility, I now choose to consider others more significant than myself. I choose to honour God and honour other leaders. I choose to rest in God's sovereignty over my life and my leadership, rejoicing that my name is written in heaven. Amen.

Note: If you are using the accompanying DVD to go through this process, the notes for the talk that introduces Step 7 are on pages 129–132.

Step Seven: Choosing Faith For Leading

Unbelief is another sin that acts like a cancer for leadership. Unbelief is not the same as doubt. Doubt, a sense of uncertainty, is common to all people. The Bible tells us to be merciful to those who doubt (Jude 22). Unbelief is the opposite of faith, resistant and hostile towards belief. Unbelief undermines our confidence in God and leads us away from the truth. Unbelief blinds our minds and hardens our hearts. As leaders we must repent of our unbelief and be transformed by the renewing of our minds.

Faith is a state and act of believing on the basis of the reliability of the one trusted. Faith depends on relationship with the object of faith. (In the New Testament, "faith", "belief", and "trust" generally flow from the same word, which can be either a noun or a verb.) Faith is never blind, but depends fully on the dependability, capability, and nature of the object of faith. Faith has no power in itself; its effect flows from the power and nature of the object of faith.

Healthy leadership confidence flows from a faith in God that opens our hearts and minds to the full range of possibilities for how God might act in our leadership context. Having faith in God for leading – no matter whether the context is the Church or the marketplace – awakens us to the surprises of God's providence in our lives and the potential for God to work in any situation to bring about beneficial outcomes. Faith enlivens our leadership with joy and hope.

Begin to identify unbelief in your life with this prayer:

Dear Heavenly Father,

You have warned us to take care that we do not develop an evil, unbelieving heart that would cause us to fall away from You (Hebrews 3:12ff.). You have told us to be exhorted every day by one another and Your Word, so that we will not become hardened by the deceitfulness of sin. You have challenged us to keep our eyes fixed on Jesus so that we might hold our confidence throughout our lives (Hebrews 12:1ff.). Although I have been saved by grace through faith in Jesus Christ, faith that You have given me, I have not always applied that faith to my daily life. Although I am a believer, I have often lived practically as an

unbeliever. Although I am a Christian leader, I have often led without reference to You. Please reveal to my mind all the ways that unbelief has infected my life, so that I might repent. In Jesus' name. Amen.

Some common manifestations of unbelief:

Prayerlessness

- ❑ I do not take time every day to read the Bible and pray.
- ❑ I do not pray as much every day as God would like me to pray.
- ❑ When I encounter someone who is unwell, praying for them is not the first thing that comes to my mind or my first response.
- ❑ I do not intercede for others daily.
- ❑ I often forget to pray for someone when I said I would pray for them.
- ❑ I do not regularly pray for people to become Christians.
- ❑ When I say "grace" for a meal, I often find myself praying longer than I should.
- ❑ I do not regularly pray for those I am leading.
- ❑ I do not always pray before making key leadership decisions.
- ❑ I do not regularly pray for God to fulfil His vision for my life, ministry, work, or leadership.
- ❑ I do not ask others to pray for me as a leader.
- ❑ I do not have a sense of God's vision for my life, ministry, work, or leadership.
- ❑ Other ways that God may reveal prayerlessness to you:

Four or more ticked areas above suggests that prayerlessness is an issue.

Busyness And Hurry

- ❑ I often feel stressed because I have too many things to do.
- ❑ I often find myself walking or driving faster than I should.
- ❑ People often feel stressed and hurried when they are around me.
- ❑ People often feel that I am too busy for them.
- ❑ I get a sense of personal satisfaction from how busy I am.
- ❑ If I were not so busy, I am not sure what I would do with myself.

- ❑ I often discover that I have scheduled too many appointments in a day.
- ❑ I struggle to say "no" to new commitments and responsibilities, especially if they look really good to me.
- ❑ I do not have time to do little things for the people closest to me.
- ❑ I repeatedly fail to keep my promises and commitments to myself and others.
- ❑ I often find myself trying to make things happen.
- ❑ I often feel frustrated and irritable, especially when I think of all I need to do.
- ❑ I rarely come away from my busy life to pray and seek God.
- ❑ Other ways that God may reveal busyness and hurry to you:

Four or more ticked items above suggests that busyness and hurry are issues.

Failure To Rest

- ❑ I have difficulty slowing down.
- ❑ I often do not have or take a day off every week.
- ❑ I do not practise some kind of "Sabbath".
- ❑ I do not always take all my holidays, or I tend to take them only a few days at a time.
- ❑ I tend to stay up too late.
- ❑ I generally do not get as much sleep as I should.
- ❑ I do not have much that I enjoy doing outside of my work or ministry.
- ❑ I do not have enough time for the people who are closest to me.
- ❑ Other ways that God may reveal your failure to rest to you:

Three or more ticked items above suggests that failure to rest is an issue.

Putting One's Ministry Or Work Before Relationship With God (Idolatry)

- ❑ Although I hate to admit it, I often find myself spending so much time on ministry or work that I do not have enough time to pray, worship, and read the Bible.
- ❑ People sometimes tell me that they feel I put my ministry or work before them.
- ❑ I spend so much time doing ministry that I find it difficult to receive ministry.
- ❑ If someone examined my life, especially how I spend my time, they might struggle to see that my priorities were God first and family second.
- ❑ I often feel irritated by those who want to spend time with me, especially those close to me.
- ❑ I often feel condemned or guilty because I have not spent time with God.
- ❑ Other ways that God may reveal about how you put things before Him:

Three or more ticked items above suggests that you may be putting your ministry or work before relationship with God.

Other Manifestations Of Unbelief:

- ❑ I have trouble accepting that what God says in the Bible is true, especially for me.
- ❑ If I ordered my life according to the Bible, I would struggle to survive in this world.
- ❑ It is easier for me to apply the Bible to my personal life than my professional life.
- ❑ I often feel that the Bible may work for others but it doesn't work for me.
- ❑ I often think that God will not use me because I don't pray enough, don't know the Bible well enough, am not holy enough, or (list the reason).

- ❑ Other people's spiritual gifts, skills, or talents are more important for advancing God's kingdom than mine are.
- ❑ I do not generally sense that my leadership, ministry, or work really make any difference for God and others.
- ❑ Because of my past sins and mistakes, God will not use me like He uses other people.
- ❑ Other ways that God may reveal unbelief to you:

If you ticked any of the items above, it may suggest that unbelief is an issue. Turn away from unbelief using this prayer:

Dear Heavenly Father, Because of unbelief, Your Son Jesus could do no mighty works in Nazareth. Because of my unbelief, I have not often seen Your Son Jesus do mighty works in my life, work, ministry, and leadership. I have not always chosen the way of faith, but I have often hardened my heart and closed my mind to the truth of Your Word. I confess that my unbelief is sin. I confess the specific ways that unbelief has manifested in my life: __________(list them).

Thank You that in Jesus Christ I am forgiven. I renounce all the ways unbelief has shown itself in my life as sin. Wash me clean of unbelief. I choose to renew my mind in the truth of who You are and in the truth of Your Word.

By faith I believe that You have cleansed my heart. I receive my place among those sanctified by faith. I choose to live by faith. I thank You that I am justified by faith and redeemed by faith. I choose to walk by faith and not by sight. I choose to exercise my leadership, do my work, and serve in ministry all by faith. By faith, I choose to receive and exercise the stewardship that You have given me. By faith I choose to obey You. By faith I choose to live my life as You decide.

I thank You for the faith You have given me, knowing that even if I have faith as small as a mustard seed, I will see the mountains move and the glory of the Lord revealed in my life. Thank You, most of all, that I have been saved by Your grace through faith, faith which You have given me through Your Son Jesus Christ in the power of Your Holy Spirit. Amen.

(Acts 15:9; Acts 26:18; Romans 1:17; Romans 3:23ff.; 2 Corinthians 5:7; Galatians 2:20; 1 Timothy 1:4; Hebrews 11; Ephesians 2:8)

Declaration Of Faith

Conclude these Steps with this declaration of faith:

I here and now, in the name of the one Lord Jesus Christ, declare my faith in the living God. I declare that there is only one God who exists as the Father, Son, and Holy Spirit. He is the creator and sustainer of all things.

I declare that Jesus Christ is the Messiah, the Word who became flesh and dwelt among us. I declare that Jesus died on the cross for the forgiveness of sins and rose bodily from the dead on the third day. I declare that He came to destroy the works of the devil, and that He has disarmed the rulers and authorities and made a public display of them, having triumphed over them by the cross.

I declare that the Holy Spirit, who lives in me, is fully God, who by His indwelling presence causes people to be born again into the Kingdom of God. The Holy Spirit seals God's people until the day of redemption. By His empowering presence, the Holy Spirit enables people to live for God and extend God's loving rulership into the whole world.

I declare that I have been saved by grace through faith in Jesus Christ, and not as a result of any works on my part. I declare that God has delivered me from the dominion of darkness and transferred me to His Kingdom. I declare that I am now seated with Christ in the heavenly places as a fully adopted child of God.

I declare that apart from Christ I can do nothing, but I can do all things through Christ who strengthens me. So I declare my complete dependence on Jesus Christ. I declare to the spiritual realms that Jesus is my only Lord and Saviour.

I declare that the Bible is trustworthy and true, the only reliable standard for faith and life. I declare that the promises God makes in the Bible are dependable and the revelation of God in the Bible is faithful.

I declare that I belong to Christ for I was bought with a price. I declare my entire being to be a living sacrifice, holy and acceptable to God through Jesus. I declare that my life and my leadership, my work and my ministry, all belong to the Lord Jesus Christ and I submit them freely to Him. I declare that Christ is in me, the hope of glory.

I declare by faith that I receive the Holy Spirit as the Father has promised. I declare by faith that I will do the works that Jesus did to the glory of the Father. I declare that I will live by faith and not by sight, seeking to please and honour God in all I say and do, to the glory of Jesus Christ.

I fully commit myself to the leadership to which God has called me: __________(name or describe that leadership). I fully commit myself to loving and serving the people to whom God has called me. I fully commit myself to humble leadership within the sphere God has given me. I fully commit myself to bringing glory and honour to Jesus Christ through my leadership.

I declare that the Lord Jesus has all authority in heaven and on earth. I declare that Jesus Christ is coming soon. Jesus is the Alpha and the Omega, the beginning and the end. I declare that by His blood Jesus ransomed people for God from every tribe and language and people and nation, and He has made them a kingdom and priests to our God, and we shall reign on the earth.

I declare that holy, holy, holy is the Lord God Almighty, who was and is and is to come. I declare that worthy is the Lamb who was slain to receive power and wealth and wisdom and might and honour and glory and blessing. Amen!

(See Exodus 20:2, 3; Colossians 1:16, 17; John 1:1, 14; Colossians 2:15; 1 John 3:8; John 3:1ff.; Ephesians 1:13; Acts 1:8; Colossians 1:13, 14; Galatians 4:5–7; John 15:5–8; Philippians 4:13; 2 Timothy 3:15–17; 1 Corinthians 6:20; Romans 12:1; Luke 11:13; John 14:12; 2 Corinthians 5:7; Matthew 28:18; Revelation 22:12–13; Revelation 5:9–12.)

Next Steps – Changing Faulty Beliefs

We are transformed through the renewing of our minds. Before you finish the process, ask God to highlight for you where you need to change your belief system. What faulty beliefs has He helped you identify as you have gone through *The Steps To Freedom For Leaders*? Where do you need to do some work to renew your mind?

Pray the following prayer:

Heavenly Father,

I commit myself to living according to the truth. Thank you for revealing to me ways in which I have not been doing that. I ask you now through the Spirit of Truth to show me the key strongholds in my mind, the areas where my belief system has been faulty. I commit myself to renewing my mind so that I will be transformed and will become the person and the leader you want me to be.

In Jesus' name. Amen.

Sit in silence and write down areas where you realize your thinking has been faulty (i.e. does not line up with what God says in His Word). There is space for this on pages 190–191. Bear in mind that the faulty thinking will still *feel* true to you. It might help to look back through the Steps and the notes you have made in *Freed To Lead*.

Then pick no more than three key areas that you will commit to focus on to renew your mind and write them on pages 188–189. On the left-hand side write down the faulty belief and on the right side write what God says in His Word. Write as many verses as you can find that say what is really true.

For the first area, write a stronghold-buster along the following lines:

I renounce the lie that....

I announce the truth that.... [list the truth from the verses you found]

Declare it every day for the next 40 days or until you know that your belief system has changed. Then come back and do the same for the second one and then the third one. Imagine how much more effective you could be as a leader if you could deal completely with these issues. And you can!

Faulty Thinking (Lies)	What God Says (Truth)

Faulty Thinking (Lies)	What God Says (Truth)

Notes

www.ingramcontent.com/pod-product-compliance
Ingram Content Group UK Ltd.
Pitfield, Milton Keynes, MK11 3LW, UK
UKHW020224250726
13967UKWH00001B/170

9 781913 082260